SNAPREVISE

SnapRevise Text Guide:
Macbeth
by William Shakespeare

Alexander Poniris

InStudent Education UK Ltd owner of SnapRevise® trademark.
43 Priston Close, Worle, BS22 7FL, Weston-Super-Mare, United Kingdom

www.snaprevise.co.uk

Copyright © InStudent Publishing Pty Ltd 2024

All rights reserved. These notes are protected by copyright owned by InStudent Publishing Pty Ltd and you may not reproduce, disseminate, or communicate to the public the whole or a substantial part thereof except as permitted at law or with the prior written consent of InStudent Publishing Pty Ltd.

Title: Macbeth by William Shakespeare Text Guide
ISBN: 978-1-917424-28-8

Published by InStudent Education UK Ltd CN 15550989 under licence from InStudent Publishing Pty Ltd.
ACN 624 188101

Disclaimer

No reliance on warranty. These SnapRevise materials are intended to supplement but are not intended to replace or to be any substitute for your regular school attendance, for referring to prescribed texts, or for your own note taking. You are responsible for following the appropriate syllabus, attending school classes, and maintaining good study practices. It is your responsibility to evaluate the accuracy of any information, opinions, and advice in these materials. Under no circumstance will InStudent Publishing Pty Ltd or InStudent Education UK Ltd ("Publishers"), their officers, agents, or employees be liable for any loss or damage caused by your use or reliance on these materials, including any adverse impact upon your performance in any academic subject as a result of your use or reliance on the materials. You accept that all information provided or made available by the Publishers is in the nature of general information and does not constitute advice. It is not guaranteed to be error-free and you should always independently verify any information, including through use of a professional teacher and other reliable resources. To the extent permissible at law, the Publishers expressly disclaim all warranties or guarantees of any kind, whether express or implied, including without limitation any warranties concerning the accuracy or content of information provided in these materials or other fitness for purpose. The Publishers shall not be liable for any direct, indirect, special, incidental, consequential or punitive damages of any kind. You agree to indemnify the Publishers, its officers, agents, and employees against any loss whatsoever by using these materials.

Preface

Hello my name is Alexander Poniris and I am your Text Guide author for Shakespeare's tragedy *Macbeth*. First and foremost, I would like to introduce myself and some of the reasons why I am here to help you with this wonderful text. I graduated high school in 2018, so to the many of you feeling daunted about what lies ahead, feel comfortable knowing that I am someone with a fresh perspective who understands the stress, strain, and confusion of the grind that is English. I completed three English subjects in my final year, each of which helped me realise my love for Shakespeare, and specifically *Macbeth*. As a lifelong fan of horror and history, the story, setting, themes, and imagery put forth by the play gripped me immediately.

Though to some of you, the thought of studying Shakespeare seems intimidating, or just completely irrelevant to our modern context, I take it as my duty to debunk these worries, as *Macbeth* at heart is a simple and powerful story, with the ability to connect with all who read it. A tale of prophecy, treachery, and eventually war, *Macbeth*'s characters represent themes of power, corruption, and the folly of human ambition and the consequences wrought from its failure. Inspiring thousands of works of fiction in its wake, its relevance stretches east and west with films such as Kurosawa's *Throne of Blood* and novels such as George R.R Martin's *A Song of Ice and Fire* series taking great inspirations from Shakespeare's dark tragedy.

I hope you enjoy your study of *Macbeth!*

— Alexander Poniris

Contents

1. **Nutshell Summary** 1
2. **Background Information** 3
   - The real Macbeth 3
   - Kings and legacy 5
   - Witches and noble ladies 7
3. **Scene-by-Scene Analysis** 10
   - Act 1 Scene 1 10
   - Act 1 Scene 2 11
   - Act 1 Scene 3 12
   - Act 1 Scene 4 14
   - Act 1 Scene 5 14
   - Act 1 Scene 6 16
   - Act 1 Scene 7 16
   - Act 2 Scene 1 18
   - Act 2 Scene 2 19
   - Act 2 Scene 3 21
   - Act 2 Scene 4 23
   - Act 3 Scene 1 24
   - Act 3 Scene 2 25
   - Act 3 Scene 3 27
   - Act 3 Scene 4 28
   - Act 3 Scene 5 30
   - Act 3 Scene 6 32
   - Act 4 Scene 1 33
   - Act 4 Scene 2 35
   - Act 4 Scene 3 37
   - Act 5 Scene 1 39
   - Act 5 Scene 2 41
   - Act 5 Scene 3 42
   - Act 5 Scene 4 43
   - Act 5 Scene 5 43
   - Act 5 Scene 6 45
   - Act 5 Scene 7 46
   - Act 5 Scene 8 46
   - Act 5 Scene 9 48

4 Character Analysis — 50
- Macbeth — 50
- Lady Macbeth — 51
- Duncan — 53
- Macduff — 54
- Banquo — 55
- The Witches — 56
- Malcolm — 57
- The Thanes — 57
- The Murderers — 58
- Lady Macduff — 58
- Hecate — 59
- Fleance — 59
- Siward and Young Siward — 60

5 Key Themes Analysis — 61
- Power — 61
- Ambition — 62
- Violence — 63
- Destiny — 64
- Guilt — 65
- Gender — 66

6 Structural Features Analysis — 67
- Motifs — 67
  - Blood — 67
  - Fathers and sons — 67
  - The known and unknown — 68
- Literary form and aesthetic features — 68
  - Structure — 68
  - Tragedy — 70
  - Verse and meter — 71
  - Dramatic irony — 72
  - Imagery — 72

7 Quote Bank — 73
- Power — 73
- Ambition — 74
- Violence — 75
- Destiny — 76
- Guilt — 77
- Gender — 78
- Supernatural — 79

8 Sample Essays — 81
- Essay One — 81
- Essay Two — 86
- Essay Three — 90
- Essay Four — 94

Section 1

Nutshell Summary

Set in medieval Scotland, *Macbeth's* story begins as it ends: **with Scotland at war and foul play in the air.** Opening in the midst of a storm, three mysterious witches meet and plot their dark plan involving a man known as Macbeth, who is **kin** to the king of Scotland, Duncan. Macbeth's title is **Thane** of Glamis, and he is a highly capable warrior, as seen when it is revealed Macbeth has succeeded in ending the rebellion against Duncan's rule.

After the battle, Macbeth and his fellow thane Banquo encounter the **three mysterious witches** who begin to tell prophecies of great fortune to both men. To Macbeth they tell of a great rise to power, promising him that he will first become Thane of Cawdor and then eventually king of Scotland. They also tell Banquo that although he will not be king, his line will **beget** kings. The witches vanish into thin air, and Macbeth and Banquo doubt what they have been told until a messenger from King Duncan confirms Macbeth as the new Thane of Cawdor after the previous thane died in the rebellion. Now believing wholeheartedly in the prophecy, Macbeth he agrees to Duncan's request to host a feast at Macbeth's castle at Inverness where Lady Macbeth receives the news and begins to plot her and her husband's ambitious ascent.

Once the royal party arrives, **Lady Macbeth conspires with her husband to murder Duncan** and take his place as king, at first admonishing Macbeth for his reluctance to fulfil his ambition. During the night while the King is sleeping, Macbeth sneaks into his chamber and murders him.

The next morning, in the presence of lords, Macbeth blames the King's death on two drunk servants who Macbeth kills to hide his guilt. Noting the absence of the King's sons Malcolm and Donalbain, Macbeth shifts blame upon them and declares himself as the rightful king of Scotland, thus fulfilling the prophecy.

Kin: a relative or family member.

Thane: an old Scottish term for a nobleman who owned land.

Beget: to father a child; to bring about offspring.

Yet as swift as Macbeth's rise to power is, his downfall is equally abrupt. To secure his power, and with the death of King Duncan still being seen as suspicious, Macbeth begins to fear Banquo's side of the prophecy, since he assumes Banquo's sons will one day kill him to take the throne. After Banquo and his son leave Macbeth's castle one night, the new king hires murderers to slay Banquo and his son Fleance. Only succeeding in killing Banquo, Macbeth briefly feels at peace until the ghost of Banquo appears at a feast sitting in Macbeth's chair, only seen by Macbeth himself. Madly raving at thin air, more suspicion grows as Macbeth begins to **descend deeper into paranoia.** Once again he consults the witches, who tell him to beware of the thane Macduff. However, they seemingly **allay** his worries, promising that no mortal man born from a woman can kill Macbeth, and that he will not be defeated until the forest of Birnam Wood moves upon his castle. Satisfied, Macbeth sends more murderers to kill Macduff's wife and children. Meanwhile, Macduff meets with Prince Malcolm who leads an English army to defeat Macbeth and claim his rightful throne. Using branches from Birnam Wood to disguise themselves, the army sneaks upon Macbeth's castle, as more and more men abandon him.

Allay: to put at ease, or to minimise concerns.

Lady Macbeth, **delusional from guilt,** mysteriously dies (though it is heavily implied that she commits suicide), and **Macbeth laments the folly of his ambition.** Meeting Macduff in battle, Macbeth brags he is invincible as no man is not born from a woman can kill him... until Macduff reveals he was taken from his mother's womb (i.e. a cesarean birth), and Macduff subsequently beheads Macbeth. Presenting the head to Malcolm, the young prince is then decreed as the new king of Scotland.

Section 2

Background Information

In order to truly understand *Macbeth* as a text, much like the study of many others, viewing and learning about what inspired the play can help to not only give more weight to the text's themes, story, and characters, but also aid in understanding some of the more difficult to understand aspects of Shakespeare's writing. With a text as deep and complex as *Macbeth*, in order to effectively understand its full context, this section will be broken down into various sections discussing not only the historical context of the play's setting and story but also the socio-political context of Shakespeare himself and period in which he wrote *Macbeth*.

The real Macbeth

Though having fantastical elements of magic, prophecy, and the supernatural, the namesake of the play and his bloody takeover of the crown of Scotland are very much real and **steeped in rich and violent history.** The real King Macbeth was assumed to have born around 1005 CE, and unlike the twisted, guilt-ridden figure we follow throughout the play, was seemingly a normal man of his time. Born in the region of Alba, historians from his time describe Macbeth during his youth as handsome, tall, and fair-haired with royal connections from birth (as it is probable he was the cousin of King Malcolm the Second). Before moving deeper into Macbeth's life, it is prudent to analyse the socio-political state of the Scotland Macbeth would rule. By understanding this, we will not only gain more insight into the text's purpose, but we will also learn just how realistic the violence Shakespeare demonstrates in the play truly is.

As said before, the real King Macbeth was born in the region of Alba, governed by semi-independent rulers known as **mormaers.** Though believed to be autonomous, historians have speculated that they came under the general control of a high king of Scotland, a position held by King Malcolm II. The whole confusion about the governance of Scotland at this time arises due to the fact that an incredible amount of internal rebellion and violence against neighbouring regions occurred regularly. Macbeth's family ruled the region of Moray, with his father Findlay sending raiding parties into Alba directly against the rule of King Malcolm II. King Malcolm himself cut a bloody path to the kingship, murdering all rival claimants to his throne. To make even more clear the chaotic state that Scotland's political system was in during the 11th and 12th centuries, before Malcolm II came to the throne, the heir to the high king was not his son, but rather, his brother. This was due to the large number of rulers being killed by rivals, and the fact it would clean up the number of claimants to the throne borne from sons and grandsons.

Mormaer: the old Scottish equivalent of an earl, or as in this play, a 'thane.'

All this information is important to understand as it puts into perspective the world Macbeth was not only born into but would one day rule. Critics contemporary to Shakespeare's time would often criticise the obscene levels of violence within his plays marking it as unrealistic, yet with a modern historical understanding it is more than clear that the brutal and near constant cycle of murder presented within *Macbeth* was accurate.

Such context also provides an insight into the inspiration for Shakespeare's portrayal of the real Macbeth. Macbeth's father was ruler of Moray, yet was usurped and murdered by his cousin, a man known by the name Gille Coemgain. Gille would marry a Scottish princess named Grouch, who descended from the royal line Malcolm deposed, giving himself and his children a claim to the high kingship. But history is nothing if not tragic and bloody – in 1032, Gille Coemgain and nearly fifty of his supporters were locked in a wooden hall and burned to death in order to depose him from power. Though it is only speculative, the likely culprit was Macbeth, who had much to gain by the murder. Not only would this act have avenged his father's death, but it also would have removed all opposition to gaining absolute power in the Moray region, as Macbeth wedded the now widowed Grouch to shrewdly gain the claim to the high-kingship much like his now dead rival had. If true, the brutal disposal of enemies and quick political manoeuvring by the real Macbeth fits nicely with his murderous fictional counterpart, with the bloody slaughter of Macduff's family and the assassination of Banquo possibly being inspired by this single act of bloody vengeance. The claim made earlier that the real Macbeth was not some twisted fictional character may seem false with this new information, but as established with the context stated before, all that Macbeth did was typical for a man in his position, and his actions would be ones in a long and common line passed down for generations to come.

After coming to the rule of Moray, Macbeth began his campaign to rule all of Scotland, by first invading the region to the north before meeting Malcolm II's grandson and new high king of Scotland, Duncan I, in battle. Unlike the peaceful and seemingly prosperous rule shown in Shakespeare's play where Duncan is a strong and well-liked leader, the real King Duncan was seen by his contemporaries as ineffective, weak, and unworthy king. The real Duncan perished in the battlefield in 1040, not slaughtered in his sleep by a scheming Macbeth. By right of conquest and bloodline, Macbeth was crowned unopposed with Duncan's son Malcolm fleeing the country much like in the play. Though not done within the shadows, secrecy, and treachery displayed within the play it is clear that **both the real and fictionalised routes to power were paved with extreme violence.** Though this violence and unlawful seizure of the crown leads to paranoia and madness to befall Macbeth and his rule, in reality, Macbeth's reign was one that brought peace, prosperity, and international awareness not seen before in Scotland, for the near decade that he ruled. Macbeth even made a pilgrimage to Rome by invitation of the Pope; hence, historians agree that Macbeth's Scotland was one politically and financially secure enough to manage such a journey.

Yet, as seemingly peaceful as Macbeth's rule was, much like so many kings before him, his reign it came to a brutal and violent end. Mirroring the play, Duncan's son, Malcolm, invaded Macbeth's Scotland with an English army lead by Siward, Earl of Northumbria. Though there is no mention of the invading army using branches of Birnam Wood to disguise themselves, the Battle of Dunsinane Hill was just as vicious as its fictional counterpart, with total casualties numbering over 4,000 (3,000 of whom were Scottish). The real Macbeth did not perish in this battle, however; but it was a decisive and destructive loss with a large chunk of his kingdom now belonging to Malcolm. Whatever hope the old king had when news of Siward's death came was brief; seeking vengeance for his father, Malcolm once again invaded Scotland in 1057, uniting Macbeth's old enemies to the north in a final push to depose him. At the Battle of Lumphanan, cornered and surrounded by new and old enemies, **Macbeth I, High King of Scotland died as he had lived: violently!** Some historians theorise that much like Macbeth was the one to kill Duncan, Malcolm delivered the killing blow to the man who killed his father. Though a fitting possible end, many historians dismiss this as overly romantic and more fitting of the play than real history. Regardless, after putting down Macbeth's step-son's claim to the throne, Malcolm, son of King Duncan, was crowned rightful and undisputed high king of Scotland, ending a decade of rule under Macbeth.

When comparing the real history to the text, it is clear that much of what Shakespeare wrote about the tragic king of Scotland is a lot closer to fact than what is generally assumed. Though not a complete monster, Macbeth's violent and arguably unlawful take over of the crown and his eventual demise at the hands of those he deposed is innately poetic, and when considering the history and society of Macbeth's Scotland, entirely predictable. It is in this predictability and historical poetry that Shakespeare must have taken inspiration. The almost definite formula and nature of his tragedies that will be explained further on fits beautifully with the seemingly endless struggle for power that plagued 11th century Scotland. Certain characters may be missing, with no mention of a Macduff, Banquo, or even a scheming version of Lady Macbeth, and absolutely no supernatural factors, the events and people at the heart of the story are clearly inspired by history and then interwoven with Shakespeare's own creativity.

Kings and legacy

Although it's interesting to consider the historical origins of Shakespeare's tragedy and the life of the real Macbeth, what's more important for our studies is understanding the world the text was created in and performed for. The figure of Shakespeare himself is a complex one, and a detailed analysis of his life up until *Macbeth* isn't entirely necessary. What is useful, however, is addressing the highly dynamic social and political climate England was undergoing before, during, and after *Macbeth*'s release, and the ways Shakespeare himself capitalised on this within the play.

First and foremost, the issue of royalty must be addressed, as their influence is deeply linked to Shakespeare's history and works. For many years Shakespeare's greatest and most influential patron was Queen Elizabeth I of England. Her rule in modern culture today is almost defined by her connection to Shakespeare as it was during her reign that he had released the bulk of his productions.

Shakespeare's works were part of a wave of new culture and learning that would become synonymous with the **Tudor era** of England. Scholars and historians agree that many of the plays Shakespeare released during Elizabeth's reign were lighter hearted, with examples including *A Midsummer's Night Dream* and *Twelfth Night*, as well as plays detailing and glorifying Elizabeth's family's rise to power with examples found in *Richard III* and *Henry VIII*. What is observed here is that Shakespeare, even from his earliest works, was incredibly politically aware, not only capitalising on the wave of prosperity brought by Elizabeth but constantly keeping in the good graces of the royal family, ensuring his continued success and more importantly **patronage**. This is important to establish, as by the time *Macbeth* had been written, Shakespeare used these same methods to curry favour with Elizabeth's successor: **King James VI of Scotland** (a.k.a. **James I of England**).

> Patronage: to pay someone money by sponsoring their activities (in this context, the royals were patrons who funded Shakespeare's productions).

King James is a central figure to our understanding of *Macbeth*'s context, as it is rumoured that the play was written specifically in honour of him. Ascending to the English throne in 1603, James became king of a foreign country with foreign beliefs. Elizabeth left no direct heirs, so through tracing the family line, James was found as a distant relative. Unlike Elizabeth, who was an open and progressive queen, James was highly superstitious and held specific spiritual beliefs regarding the supernatural; this impacts hugely on many of the themes of *Macbeth,* especially the notion of witches. Before becoming King of England and while ruling Scotland, King James came to believe that a coven of witches was plotting to murder him. Though this seems far-fetched today, there was a severe lack of understanding of the natural world in James I's time, and so he attempted to quash these rumours with brutal action. A series of witch trials occurred in 1591 leading to the imprisonment and death of those accused of witchcraft, the majority of whom were women. King James took his belief and fear of witches even further by publishing a book on witchcraft in 1597 called *Daemonologie* to serve as guide to identify and deal with suspected witches.

It isn't a surprise then that witches appear in *Macbeth* and their mysterious and dark magic leads to Macbeth's demise. To his audience, this would have served as a powerful reminder of the dangers that witchcraft presented, as well as fuelling the drama of the play by feeding off their superstition and fear. Yet the connections go deeper when analysing the growth of such heavy, superstitious beliefs around the time King James took the throne. It was no coincidence that the wave of belief in witches and dark forces occurred at a time in which a new ruler had suddenly and contentiously came to the English throne. Time and time again, historians have observed that times of political instability and turmoil often caused a renewed interest and concern with witchcraft, reflecting the societal anxiety present when change was brought to their often closed-off worlds.

In the case of King James, his ascendancy wasn't smooth, as England had experienced a century of Tudor rule was now suddenly ruled by not only someone they had no prior knowledge of, but a *foreigner* as well! The infamous Gunpowder Plot of 1605 in which an assassination of King James was planned but ultimately foiled reflected the highly tense and delicate nature of England during this time. By the time Shakespeare realised his play in 1606, he had more than enough knowledge to craft something perfect to gain favour with the tense and superstitious king. As well as playing off the superstitious nature of James, Shakespeare cleverly made sure to make reference to his Scottish heritage, specifically regarding James' right to rule. The witches inform us that Banquo's descendants will be kings one day, and historically, King James' family claimed to be descended from Banquo's son, the legendary Fleance, giving them a form of **divine right** to rule Scotland. Though highly disputed by modern historians as there is little to no mention of a Banquo or Fleance in the real Macbeth's life, during the 17th century such a connection was incredibly important in ensuring the absolute power James held as King of Scotland. By creating a play centred on Scottish politics and the theme of a true king coming to power by divine right, it appears that Shakespeare cleverly gave public praise and support to King James, spreading this sentiment throughout society as both the nobility and commonfolk flocked to see Shakespearean productions.

Divine right of kings: the belief that kings are appointed by God.

Much like the history of the real Macbeth, understanding the context surrounding society at the time of the play's release offers insight into many of the themes and motives Shakespeare had when creating it. The struggle for power, the heavy supernatural atmosphere, and the consequences for wrongly attempting to **usurp** power found within *Macbeth* all have their roots within this context. Understanding this not only makes it easier to interpret the play's themes and characters, but also gives a greater appreciation for the text itself.

Usurp: to seize a position of power by force.

Witches and noble ladies

Within the majority of Shakespeare's texts, the representation of women in varied and diverse positions of power is unfortunately lacking. Portrayed mostly as love interests and plot drivers, unlike the men of their respective stories, women find little time to shine in Shakespeare's plays, but *Macbeth* is a notable exception. Though the role *Macbeth*'s women in the plot will be discussed further in the thematic study (see page 66), it is important to bring up the unusual portrayal of women in the play here so that we may search for answers in Shakespeare's socio-cultural context.

First, let's talk about the witches. The idea of witchcraft during the time of *Macbeth*'s creation and release was **pervasive** in English and Scottish culture. Believed to have been wicked women who consorted and made pacts with demons and even the devil himself, **witches were seen as the ultimate corruption of what a woman should be** during that period.

Pervasive: widespread, extensive, or deeply entrenched.

Highly sexualised, witches symbolised temptation and vanity, often cursing those who had done the most minor wrong to them and bringing great misfortune to all who dared seek them. Though in hindsight the notion of witches even being real is ridiculous, to the 17th century people of England, a country in the grips of strong, spiritual beliefs, witches represented all that the Bible warned against. In more speculative terms, they also represented the fear many held of the natural world around them, and the often heartbreaking and mysterious tragedies that would befall them seemingly out of nowhere. In times of political instability, the superstitions surrounding witches seem to spike, which makes sense considering that the common people had very little political or social knowledge, so would naturally attribute the completely chaotic political events to something powerful and difficult to fathom. Scholars see this as a coping mechanism to change, and hence Shakespeare included ideas of witchcraft in his play as the bloody chaos that consumes Macbeth, Duncan, and all of Scotland **germinate** from a prophecy granted by witches.

Germinate: to cause something to grow, like sprouting a seed.

Being creatures of supernatural origin and ability, witches throughout history are often depicted to have some future telling abilities, with specific examples being the visions of the Oracle of Delphi from Ancient Greek legend, or the more common image of a witch peering into a crystal ball. What matters to this context is that **Shakespeare depicts these prophetic abilities at the centre of the witches' role within the play,** as not only do the witches correctly predict Macbeth's rise to power, they also later ominously foreshadow his downfall. It is curious that Shakespeare placed such power in the hands of women when considering his context, as when looking at the play as a whole, it is the witches' actions that catalyse the events of the play – from the murder of Duncan to the devastation of civil war. Shakespeare is not only demonstrating the power believed to have been held by these women during the 17th century, but reaffirms the danger and fear they caused to those who believed in their existence, such as King James.

We should also analyse how Shakespeare portrays women of noble birth in the play, specifically Lady Macbeth and Lady Macduff. To start with, it is clear that Lady Macbeth is portrayed in an antagonistic light throughout the play, and other than the witches, she is the main driving force behind the crimes Macbeth commits, especially the murder of Duncan, as she is the one to formulate the plan. Much like the witches, it is clear that Lady Macbeth's cruelty, wickedness, and eventual guilt-ridden downfall were warnings to the general public. However, it is curious that while portraying Lady Macbeth in such a light, Shakespeare never portrays her as lesser than Macbeth. In fact, although Macbeth is the ruler in name, it is Lady Macbeth who serves as the politician, carefully planning her husband's ascent and reigning him in when his madness begins. Contextually, for centuries of English history, women were expected to be domestic wives and mothers, so it is strange that Lady Macbeth is given such prominent and visual political power.

To turn back to the real Macbeth briefly, his real wife Grouch's perspective is sadly neglected, and all we know is the only true power she held was her bloodline to the high-kingship of Scotland – something controlled by the men who married her. For years, Shakespeare had written plays and tried to garner favour with a powerful female monarch, Queen Elizabeth I, and would have been exposed to the reality of rule under a woman. Yet unlike Lady Macbeth, who was written as cruel and cold, historians account that Elizabeth was a just and fair ruler, doing much to benefit the country as a whole rather than herself. Elizabeth was dead by the time the play was written, however; and James was king, but he had his own connection to a powerful female monarch, one that Shakespeare could exploit in order to gain more favour with the king: his mother, Mary I of Scotland, or Mary, Queen of Scots.

Cousin to Queen Elizabeth, Mary, Queen of Scots is a curious figure in history. Rising to the throne at only six days old, Mary spent much of her life in France and would soon marry Francis II of France. It was only after her husband's death in 1560 that returned home to Scotland and begin to rule as queen. Mary's rule was troubled by various political and religious issues, yet historians note she was a cunning and clever ruler who held great independence, seen within her search for a new royal husband, as she denied and outright dismissed many potential husbands put forth by her advisors. Eventually marrying her first cousin, the Lord of Darnley, and giving birth to James I of England, her power began to wane as the mysterious death of her husband in an explosion and her subsequent remarriage to the man believed to have been responsible, led to her forced abdication and exile to England. There, believing she would find support with her cousin Elizabeth, Mary was seen as an even greater threat as she potentially held a claim to the English throne and was imprisoned by Elizabeth for nearly eighteen years before being executed on charges of treason in 1587, after supposedly planning to assassinate Queen Elizabeth.

Now understanding who Mary was, it is easy to see how Shakespeare could gain favour with King James by portraying women with power in a certain way in his play. Though this is all speculative, it is easy to make connections between Mary, Queen of Scots and Lady Macbeth through a modern understanding, but considering the ruler and time period, Lady Macduff would have been a better suited counterpart. Lady Macduff, whose character will be discussed in more depth later, through a historical lens, is the ideal noblewoman of *Macbeth*'s context. Loyal and devoted to raising her children right, Lady Macduff embodies the values a good woman was expected to have during the 17th century of honesty, devotion, and selflessness while maintaining a strong moral and mental state. It is possible that Shakespeare was attempting to make a royal connection to James to remind the new monarch of his powerful mother. Once again this is all speculative and should not be taken as hard fact, but is plausible when considering how Shakespeare manipulated politics in crafting his plays.

Macbeth presents us with both positive and negative female characters who shape its tragic and violent story, so understanding these women is essential for our grasp of the text's key ideas. By considering the real life influences and inspirations behind characters like Lady Macbeth, Lady Macduff, and the witches, we can glean a greater understanding of what Shakespeare was intending when composing the play.

Section 3
Scene-by-Scene Analysis

Act 1 Scene 1
Scene Summary
The play opens with thunder and lightning, and three witches arrive in the middle of a storm. They discuss when they should meet again, deciding to meet when a battle is "lost and won," and to meet someone called Macbeth. Calling upon their **familiars,** they leave while ominously chanting "fair is foul, and foul is fair" before mysteriously vanishing.

Familiar: a magical demon in the form of an animal that accompanies a witch.

Scene Analysis
There is much to break down with the opening scene of the play. Almost immediately, the audience introduced to the dark nature of the text, as it opens in the midst of a storm, potentially foreshadowing the chaos later to come. Such striking imagery is complemented by the introduction of *Macbeth*'s first characters: the witches. From the start, Shakespeare has written the three witches in an incredibly mysterious and uncomfortable manner, hinting at themes of the supernatural and the danger it brings. Their language in this scene emphasises this fact, making little sense, with quotes such as "when the hurly-burly's done," and "fair is foul and foul is fair, hover through the fog and filthy air." This also foreshadows how twisted reality will become, as the natural order of Scotland is about to be disrupted.

Other than hinting at the dark times to come, this scene also introduces Macbeth, though he doesn't yet appear. Though only his name is mentioned, his importance is established almost immediately to the audience, as not only is the play named after him, but these witches, who have been presented as dark and powerful beings who foreshadow doom, wish to meet with him. It is clear that from the very beginning that Shakespeare has purposely linked the witches to Macbeth's character arc. When considering the opening scenes of Shakespeare's other tragedies, *Macbeth*'s stands out, as unlike in *Hamlet* and *Othello* (which also foreshadow the tragedy to come, sometimes with supernatural elements), *Macbeth*'s is uniquely more atmospheric and heavier in its tone. The opening scene of any of Shakespeare plays is crucial to understand, as it is the first time the audience is brought into the play's world and story, and in the case of *Macbeth*, the use of witches as characters, the vague mention of the main character's name, and eerie atmosphere created establish *Macbeth*'s setting and tone as one of mystery and darkness.

Act 1 Scene 2

Scene Summary

The scene opens with a meeting between King Duncan of Scotland, his two sons Malcolm and Donalbain, and Lennox, a thane. A bloody captain approaches them with news of the rebellion, telling King Duncan that the rebel thane Macdonald has been defeated and slain in battle by Macbeth, who is revealed to be Duncan's cousin. The captain further tells of Macbeth's bravery, defeating Macdonald's Norwegian ally with his fellow thane Banquo. Sending the man off to be healed, King Duncan receives more news as the thanes Ross and Angus enter, telling him of the victory they won against Macdonald's ally, the Thane of Cawdor. Looking to reward Macbeth, Duncan grants him the title of Thane of Cawdor, stating "what hath lost, noble Macbeth hath won," tasking Ross to deliver the news.

Scene Analysis

After the mysterious and supernatural nature of the opening scene, this scene acts as the audience's first real introduction to *Macbeth*'s Scotland and serves to establish characters and events that become crucial to the play's central conflict. To start with the characters, this is our first introduction to King Duncan and his sons Malcolm and Donalbain, with Malcolm in particular being one of the more prominent characters, as he is the one to avenge his father and defeat Macbeth at climax of the play. Yet in this scene, Malcolm barely speaks; he only introduces the captain. The audience gains a brief sense of his character as his line "who like a good and hardy solider fought... hail brave friend" mirrors the noble personality displayed by Duncan in this scene. Furthermore, Duncan is portrayed as a man of honour and kindness – he freely praises the bravery of Macbeth and Banquo, and generously gifts Macbeth an additional lordship, making him one of the most powerful men in Scotland.

It appears that Shakespeare wrote Duncan this way to highlight the evil of his murder and the villainous nature of Macbeth and his wife, but another interpretation is that this generous and trusting nature of the king can ominously be seen as a contributing factor to his downfall. As stated in the text, Duncan rewards Macbeth with the title of Thane of Cawdor, as the previous thane who held this position was a traitor to the crown, actively trying to overthrow Duncan. The granting of this title on Macbeth is a clear example of dramatic irony; as seen in the next scene, the witches will foretell that Macbeth will become Thane of Cawdor and then king, which sets Macbeth's destructive ambition in motion. Hence, Duncan's **naïvete** seemingly contributes to his own downfall, as with many of Shakespeare's tragic characters. Both Duncan and Macbeth share a **hamartia** – for Duncan it is his trusting nature, and for Macbeth it is his ambition.

Naïvete: lack of experience, wisdom, or judgement.

Hamartia: a fatal flaw that brings about negative consequences for a character.

It is also important to note, once again, that Macbeth does not physically appear in this scene; he is only named and talked about (another common technique Shakespeare uses for the **eponymous** characters in his tragedies). Though we gain a better sense of his character, Shakespeare has intentionally created an air of mystique around his enigmatic main character, a technique that heightens the tension for the rest of the play.

> **Eponymous:** a character whose name is the title of the text (e.g. Macbeth, Othello, Hamlet).

Act 1 Scene 3

Scene Summary

Amidst a thundering sky, the three witches once again meet. They discuss the mischief and evil they have been up to since their last meeting while they await the arrival of Macbeth. Hearing the noise of drums, they know it is time as they arise and welcome the new Thane of Cawdor. Macbeth arrives with his fellow thane and friend Banquo, and the two are at first shocked and disgusted by what they see, with Banquo remarking that the witches "look not like th'inhabitants o'th'earth." When Macbeth demands them to speak, they tell him a prophecy. The first hails him as "Thane of Glamis," the second as "Thane of Cawdor," and the third declares he shall be "king hereafter." Banquo, sceptical, questions the witches as to why they ignore him, and he challenges them to look into his own future. Granting him his wish, they tell Banquo that he will paradoxically be "lesser than Macbeth and greater," and that though he will not be king, his descendants shall be. Macbeth not convinced by the witches' promises, he claims he cannot be Thane of Cawdor because he believes the current Thane of Cawdor is still alive. Macbeth demands more answers, but the three witches vanish into thin air as the thanes Ross and Angus arrive to bring news from King Duncan. They inform Macbeth of his new title (surprise, it's Thane of Cawdor!) and he learns of the previous thane's **treason** and eventual capture. After talking with the thanes, Macbeth and Banquo take a moment to discuss the witches' prophecies, with Macbeth unnerved about what their claim that he will be king means. Eventually deciding to discuss it later, Macbeth summons the others and begins to ride towards the king.

> **Treason:** a crime against one's country or ruler.

Scene Analysis

Macbeth and Banquo's meeting with the witches is the first crucial scene of the play. Not only is it the first time Macbeth appears as a character, but it also introduces the sole reason behind his dark and twisted reign of terror that defines the play. By limiting the audience's exposure to Macbeth until now, Shakespeare creates an aura of mystery, and though our initial perception is one of a heroic, capable, and loyal warrior, this will soon be eroded as we witness Macbeth succumb to the witches' "suggestions" and he descends into violent paranoia and selfishness.

The establishment of Macbeth's character aside, this scene also serves to set up some major themes and conflicts going forward in the play's world. It is in this scene that Shakespeare first truly introduces the ideas of **destiny, ambition, and prophecy** and foreshadows once more the consequences lying in wait because of them. Though the first scene in the play is the audience's first exposure to the supernatural, it is in scene three that its true significance is made clear, as the prophecies spoken by the witches in hindsight are the catalysts for Macbeth's rise and fall and the period of chaos of which Scotland endures throughout the play. However, in addition to Macbeth's prophecy that is crucial to his character and the overall story, we also have Banquo's prophecy of being "lesser than Macbeth and greater... thou shalt get kings but thou be none." Though not as explicitly powerful as Macbeth's guarantee to the throne, the subtleties of this prophecy hold great meaning and power. Initially, it appears Banquo's prophecy was a contextual reference to King James' real claims to be descended from Banquo, yet when considering what Shakespeare is trying to convey through his use and portrayal of the supernatural, Banquo's prophecy is at the core of Macbeth's corruption.

Shakespeare makes it clear that **magic and witches are to be feared and whoever dabbles with them is destined for a dark path,** clearly depicted as Macbeth in this scene, for it is Macbeth's interpretation of Banquo's prophecy and the threat it may have to his own **tenuous**, fragile power which leads to the murder and attempted murder of Banquo and his son and heir Fleance. The murder of Banquo demonstrates the power prophecy has, as the mere hint of Banquo's family becoming royalty is enough to make Macbeth act violently in a desperate attempt to maintain his own promise of power, a pattern that will emerge throughout the scenes to come. It is the first time we see the idea of the **self-fulfilling prophecy** which we will break down in more detail later. For now, suffice it to say that much like the meaning behind the themes of destiny, the notion of a self-fulfilling prophecy has its roots here in the scenes with the witches.

Tenuous: something very weak or slight.

Self-fulfilling prophecy: a prediction that becomes reality because a person believes in it.

The foreshadowing in this scene is also important to discuss. Beyond the prophecies literally predicting the events to come, we also see the beginnings of Macbeth's emotional investment in the prophecies as he is told he will become one of the most powerful men in Scotland. It's also possible that Macbeth's betrayal of Duncan is foreshadowed in his receiving the position of Thane of Cawdor, as the previous man to hold the title had been in open rebellion against Duncan's kingship. Hence, both characters that hold the title of 'Thane of Cawdor' betray Duncan, with Macbeth going one step further by murdering and usurping the throne from him and his rightful heir Malcolm. Whether coincidence or not, this theory serves as another example of foreshadowing and potentially an argument in favour of the idea that Macbeth's prophecies were self-fulfilling and not magical in nature.

Act 1 Scene 4

Scene Summary

The play returns to Duncan who has just received the news of the previous Thane of Cawdor's execution via his son Malcolm. They briefly discuss the nature of death before finally receiving Macbeth and Banquo, fresh from their encounter with the witches. Duncan gives great praise to Macbeth, stating they owe him much more than they can realistic give him. Macbeth responds loyally, claiming all he did was for Duncan and his loyalty to the crown. In a state of pride and happiness due to the great victory they all achieved, Duncan announces before his "sons, kinsmen and thanes" that his son, Malcolm, is to be named Prince of Cumberland and heir apparent to the throne.

He then tells Macbeth to invite everyone to Macbeth's castle in Inverness to honour Macbeth for the great victories he has won. Speaking to himself, Macbeth becomes anxious of the king's announcement, seeing Malcolm's promotion to the Prince of Cumberland as a threat to his own supposed destiny.

Scene Analysis

The opposite of the previous scene, this part of the of the act is tonally lighter and holds much less importance to the overall story and themes of the play. This establishing scene mostly serves to bring Macbeth and Duncan together, and to begin to hint at Macbeth's paranoia about his position. Like the previous scenes, there is also some subtle foreshadowing here, as Duncan and Malcolm's conversation about the death and loyalty of the previous Thane of Cawdor ironically underscores Macbeth's future betrayal of both of them. This conversation gives further weight to the idea that the position of Thane of Cawdor is a dark symbol of betrayal, death, and usurpation.

Act 1 Scene 5

Scene Summary

A letter arrives to Inverness castle, and Lady Macbeth is introduced to the play. From Macbeth, Lady Macbeth reads about her husband's encounter with the witches, his promotion to the position of Thane of Cawdor and the prophecy that he is to become king of Scotland. Cold to her husband's word, Lady Macbeth worries about Macbeth's nature, ominously stating it is "too full o'th'milk of human kindness" to fully realise his destiny to be king. Her thoughts are interrupted by a servant telling her Macbeth and Duncan are on their way to spend the night at the castle. Telling the servant to bring Macbeth to her, she sends him away and begins to plot, calling upon dark spirits and wishing for the power remove her female nature so that she can have the strength to do what is required for Macbeth to become king. Eventually, Macbeth arrives and Lady Macbeth reveals her intention to kill King Duncan, quoting, "O never shall that morrow see," assuring her husband she has everything under control.

Scene Analysis

Though not as intense as Scene 3, this scene can be interpreted as an equally important part of Act 1. The major point to be analysed in this scene is Lady Macbeth, as for the first time the audience experience her complex and dark character. Unlike Macbeth, who has been introduced with some mystery to his true nature, Lady Macbeth is immediately cast as villainous, quoting dark words and scheming murder in order to advance herself and her husband's position of power. It is clear that Shakespeare has assigned Lady Macbeth the villainous role in the play, but curiously considering the 17th century context of the text's writing, has portrayed her with a clear sense of cunning, ambition, and intelligence. Though Macbeth is ruler of Inverness castle in a physical sense, it is apparent from the dialogue between them his wife holds great influence over his decisions, which in turn, potentially make her the true ruler of all of Macbeth's lands.

On that note, the theme of power begins to emerge in this scene, as the text reveals another form of it; unlike Macbeth's physical power through violence or Duncan's power through birthright, **Lady Macbeth displays power through manipulation,** perfectly encapsulated within her dialogue with Macbeth. A choice sequence to analyse from this scene is when Macbeth arrives with the news of the king's arrival and Lady Macbeth details her plot to kill the king. Macbeth first starts by stating the king is leave their castle tomorrow in which to his surprise Lady Macbeth responds with "O never shall sun that morrow see... your hand, your tongue; look like th'innocent flower but be the serpent underneath... give all our days and nights to come solely sovereign sway and masterdom." Macbeth is speechless after this and the effect Shakespeare intended to have on his audience would have been very similar, as Lady Macbeth's dialogue is dripping with power and intent, the complete opposite to Macbeth's doubtfulness displayed in scenes previous. Lady Macbeth's quote, though not explicitly stating the details of how to kill Duncan, seeds into Macbeth's mind the notion of murder, thus ensuring her husband's commitment to her plan.

In the male-dominated political landscape of the play's setting, this single conversation may be amongst the greatest political moves of the story, and another **catalyst** for the bloodshed to come; all accomplished by a woman. Considering the context, in Shakespeare's time this display of power would have been viewed as a negative action on Lady Macbeth's part and the destructive guilt she feels later serving as a punishment for it, from a modern analytical perspective, Lady Macbeth's speech is a beautiful example of political manipulation equal to those of her male counterparts.

Catalyst: something that sparks or precipitates an event.

There is more to dissect with Lady Macbeth however, as power isn't the only theme she introduces within this scene – we also have the issue of gender reincorporated here. As seen with the witches, the idea of women in power is almost represented as supernatural in this world, with dark tonal language and imagery used to accompany their dialogue. In the case of this scene, Lady Macbeth's quote of "unsex me here... make thick my blood, stop up th'access and passage to remorse" is the perfect example of Lady Macbeth's desire to go beyond her gender in order to pursue power. This is incredibly powerful and offers a huge insight into the character of Lady Macbeth. Though Lady Macbeth's character's relationship with power will be more carefully deconstructed later, to keep it relevant to this scene, Shakespeare has almost assigned Lady Macbeth to physically represent Macbeth's ambition. In text is appears she realises this herself as she **admonishes** Macbeth's lack of ambition present in the letter she receives stating that he is "too full o'th'milk of human kindness" and this disgust at her husband's lack of desire leads her to usurp the expectations placed on her by her own gender in order to compensate for what her husband is lacking.

Admonishes: shames or reprimands.

Act 1 Scene 6

Scene Summary

The scene opens with Duncan and Banquo arriving at Macbeth's castle of Inverness. Lady Macbeth greets them at the entrance, and Duncan inquires as to where Macbeth is. Politely, Duncan declares himself and the royal party as guests at Inverness, as he asks Lady Macbeth to lead him to her husband.

Scene Analysis

This is another minor scene, though there are few things to note here. First, again the audience gets another example of Duncan's trusting nature, and at this point the question is raised to whether such a trusting nature is a testament to Duncan's character or a detriment. Noting that Macbeth had ridden ahead mysteriously, Duncan ignores it, and for the audience who has witnessed the scene before in which Macbeth and his wife began to plot Duncan's death, this scene comes across as profoundly ironic. Moreover, Duncan's description of Lady Macbeth as a "fair and noble hostess" and the castle in which he is to meet his demise as having a "pleasant air" is almost comedic in how darkly **foreboding** it is.

Foreboding: an ominous portent of impending doom; a sense that something bad is going to happen soon.

Act 1 Scene 7

Scene Summary

Macbeth stands alone, **ruminating** on the plan to murder Duncan. Highly conflicted, he thinks if he is going to kill Duncan without consequence, it should be done quickly, yet he has the foresight to see that there will be dire consequences. He feels guilty at even the thought of murdering Duncan and the judgement to come of it, for he would not only be murdering a guest placed in his trust, but one of his own blood as well. Thinking about the good of Duncan's kingship, Macbeth is interrupted by his wife, who inquires why he has left the king's presence.

Ruminating: thinking deeply; contemplating.

Seeing his opportunity, he tells Lady Macbeth he wants nothing to do with the murder of Duncan due to the kindness and titles gifted to him. Lady Macbeth then admonishes her husband once again for his fear and lack of ambition with biting and harsh words: "art thou afeard... a coward in thine own esteem." She continues questioning Macbeth's loyalty and manhood, mocking him for his love for Duncan. Macbeth questions what will happen if they should fail in the murder, to which his wife angrily berates him, saying he should stop thinking of anything but success in their plan. She then goes on to detail how specifically the murder will play out: when the king is asleep, they will get his two servants drunk while Macbeth commits the murder, and they will blame the drunken servants when they awaken with no memory. Macbeth finally decides to go ahead with the murder as he darkly declares "false face must hide what the false heart doth know."

Scene Analysis

As the final scene of the first act, this scene is the final confirmation for what is to occur in the acts going forward for not only the audience but for the characters themselves. The plan for King Duncan's murder is finalised, and for the character of Macbeth, this scene is the end of moral struggle about becoming king, as he finally succumbs to his ambition and agrees to kill Duncan.

On that note, this scene is the most conflicted state we see Macbeth in until his "tomorrow and tomorrow" soliloquy. Here, Macbeth begins by doubting his ambition, the part of his nature driving him to even thoughts of killing Duncan. His lines "but in these cases, we still have judgement here that we but teach... which being taught, return to plague th'inventor" are greatly reflective of Macbeth's inner anxiety and guilt, and almost foreshadow his downfall to come due to the murder. Such guilt is further made clear by Shakespeare when Macbeth begins to think of Duncan's nature as a man, one displayed in previous scenes as kind, gracious, and humble in the face of victory.

He notes that "besides, this Duncan hath borne his faculties so meek, hath been so clear in his great office, that his virtues will plead like angels," once again foreshadowing Macbeth's troubled rule, as Macbeth will become the opposite king to how he describes Duncan; rather than being humble and honest, Macbeth will be despotic and murderous in order to hold power. To briefly link back to historical context, that such a dark and troubled reign would begin with the involvement of witches further conveys the dangers of trusting supernatural forces. This whole first soliloquy from a literary perspective is another example of Shakespeare's tragic irony, complex character work, and relevant use of context, as the guilt and reluctance that Macbeth ignores in order to pursue his ambition eventually leads to his downfall, eerily hinted at earlier within the text.

It is this scene that many scholars point to in the debate about whether Macbeth is a tragic hero or a true villain. It is clear to see why, as for the first and one of the only times in the play, Macbeth is shown in a deeply human light. The doubt, fear, and almost grief he feels when contemplating not only the death of his king but also "his kinsman" is incredibly poetic and lends great value and complexity to his character.

This is further displayed when Lady Macbeth enters and begins to psychological break Macbeth's character and mind in order to pursue her ambitious ends. Once again, it is clear that Shakespeare depicts Lady Macbeth as the major villain of the text as her manipulation and language within this scene drip with brutal and dark intention. Specifically, she and by extension Shakespeare play with ideas of gender and especially the roles expected of a man during *Macbeth*'s intertextual context.

To link to the real King Macbeth of Scotland, it is clear with his portrayal that Shakespeare wanted something deeper than militant warlord that is assumed to have been the real man, as all accounts from history seem to perpetuate that image. When considering the historical context of Scotland during the Middle Ages, a man was expected to fight and go to war and to take what he deemed as rightfully his. Malcolm, both in real history and the play, does just that by eventually defeating Macbeth to claim to crown and avenge his father, whereas throughout this whole scene and further towards the end of the play, Macbeth contrasts greatly with this image.

To link back to Lady Macbeth's role in this, throughout the scene, she constantly **questions Macbeth's manhood in order to rouse his ambition and pride to convince him to murder Duncan** and claim the throne and his destiny. Quotes such as "and live a coward in thine own self-esteem" and "what beast was't then that made you break this enterprise to me... be so much more the man" are examples of her frankly vicious choice of language, with the second phrase going so far to **question Macbeth's humanity,** for she is saying that only an animal would break the promise he had made to her. Shakespeare's specific choice of language for Lady Macbeth lies at the heart of his examination of gender.

Using dramatic irony, Shakespeare has twisted the expected gender roles and attitudes of Macbeth's and Lady Macbeth's context within this scene, with Macbeth being more thoughtful and cautious as expected of a noble lady in his day, whereas **Lady Macbeth is dark and almost militant in her attitude,** traits expected of Macbeth in his position. Ultimately what this twisting on gender achieves to the play overall, is to raise ideas of power, ambition, and desire, for the audience to carry with them for the acts to come.

Act 2 Scene 1

Scene Summary

Act 2 opens on a dark night with Banquo and his son, Fleance. They talk about the night as Banquo confesses he feels uneasy, telling his son "there's husbandry in heaven... a heavy summons lies lead upon me... restrain in me the cursed thoughts that nature gives way to in response." Macbeth arrives, to Banquo's surprise, and gifts Macbeth a diamond to pass on to Lady Macbeth for being such a gracious host. They talk further about the witches, and Banquo tells Macbeth he has dreamt of them and the wisdom they gave to Macbeth. Refusing to discuss them further, Macbeth requests that they should discuss this another time and dismisses him from his presence. After telling a servant to have Lady Macbeth ring a bell, he is left eventually on his own.

Alone, he has a vision of a phantom dagger within the air. Reaching out he cannot take it, blaming the "bloody business" he is to commit for it. He speaks darkly calling upon **Hecate, the goddess of the moon and magic,** to give him strength in the darkness to kill Duncan. The bell tolls, and he begins his journey to Duncan's chamber, ominously muttering about his own **deception and disloyalty** – "false face must hide what the false heart doth know" as the scene ends.

Scene Analysis

The opening of the second act begins much like the first, ominous and shrouded in mystery. Though not as blatantly gory as the scenes to follow, Shakespeare still uses dark imagery and word play here in order to create a sense of growing unease and tension. The stormy entrances of the witches, the witches themselves, and Lady Macbeth's calling upon demons to "unsex" her are all examples of Shakespeare evoking a dark and seemingly unnatural tone. Contextually, his audience would have understood the meaning of such imagery, as the deeply spiritual Jacobean masses would be wary of the fates that befell those who dabbled in unnatural forces. Shakespeare uses Banquo within this scene to reflect this notion, as he admits to his son Fleance that he feels uneasy and that something is amiss that night. Thus, Shakespeare uses Banquo as a reflection of the audience's knowledge of the darkness looming over the plot, as aside from Macbeth and Lady Macbeth, only Banquo and the audience know of Macbeth's meeting with the witches, and we are made to sympathise more with the rational and cautious Banquo over the violent and confronting Lady Macbeth.

The theme of guilt is also prominent in this scene, as Macbeth struggles with the task that lies ahead. Unlike the previous times where this has occurred, Shakespeare now visually represents the strain on Macbeth's conscience with the phantom dagger ominously floating in front of him, a powerful symbol of the murder he is going to commit. Macbeth's vision can interpret in a number of ways, each lending a deep understanding to his character. The dagger can be interpreted as just another example of magic in this world, a simple but true vision of Macbeth's task and destiny. Though valid, a deeper interpretation is that the dagger is a figment of Macbeth's slowly deteriorating mind, poisoned by ambition, fear, and greed. Although less obvious, this interpretation fits better with the overall themes of the play, and the guilt Macbeth feels at his unjust ambition. He says it himself, as when he attempts to grasp the dagger he cannot, claiming it as a "dagger of the mind, a false creation… an instrument I was to use." The link between Macbeth's guilt and the supernatural elements of the play are more common than what is first assumed, and throughout the rest of this act (and indeed the play), the idea that Macbeth's deterioration mentally is somehow linked to the disorder brought upon Scotland by his actions only becomes stronger.

Act 2 Scene 2

Scene Summary

Lady Macbeth sits in her chamber awaiting her husband's return, talking to herself about her drugging Duncan's servants so that they have no memory of what will occur during the night. Frightened by an owl's shriek, she sees Macbeth clutching two bloody daggers. She questions Macbeth if he has killed Duncan and he confirms the king is dead.

Macbeth then questions her about whether she had heard anything or if anyone has been alerted of the murder, specifically Duncan's sons. Macbeth tells his wife how the servants spoke of murder in their sleep before briefly waking and not seeing anything, though Macbeth was compelled to answer them when they began to speak a prayer. Lady Macbeth tells her husband not to think of them anymore as it will drive them both mad. Macbeth claims to have heard a voice tell him "sleep no more; Macbeth does murder sleep... Macbeth shall sleep no more."

Lady Macbeth chastises Macbeth, telling him to be braver and to stop thinking such cowardly thoughts while also instructing him to clean his hands of Duncan's blood. Realising her husband has still has the murder weapons clutched in his hand, she tells him to return them to the room, but Macbeth refuses, admitting he is afraid to witness again what he has done. Frustrated, Lady Macbeth takes the daggers from Macbeth, and angrily tells him that the sleeping and the dead are the same and nothing to be feared before leaving the room. After she leaves a mysterious knocking begins around the room, as a frightened Macbeth **questions if he can ever wash the blood off his hands** even if he were to use the ocean. Lady Macbeth returns with bloody hands herself, hearing the knocking and ordering that they both return to their bed chamber in order to wash the blood off their hands and symbolically cleanse themselves of the evil deed they have committed. She tells Macbeth not to be lost in his dark thoughts. Agreeing, Macbeth takes one last moment to reflect, remarking "to know my deed, 'twere best not know myself."

Scene Analysis

As with Macbeth's first encounter with the witches, this scene of the play is amongst its most important. All throughout the first act and the beginning of the second, Duncan's death has either been planned or foreshadowed. Great tension has been building up to this point, with Macbeth struggling with the battle between his guilt and ambition and Lady Macbeth darkly weaving the plot. So when the moment finally occurs, in true Shakespearean fashion, the audience never sees it! Much like many of Shakespeare's tragedies, certain important events are left to the audience's imagination, and are only described unreliably by the characters, leaving the audience to interpret what little information is available to them. To use another one of Shakespeare's tragedies as an example, in *Hamlet,* the death of King Hamlet is never portrayed, only mentioned by the characters in the world, with his supposed ghost being the only physical proof the audience ever witnesses of the deed. Incredibly similar is Macbeth entering the room with his two bloody daggers in this scene. Though less ambiguous than the ghost in *Hamlet*, there is still the same air of mystery present for surrounding Macbeth's murder of his king. Questions arise from this ambiguity. Did Macbeth hesitate? What emotions did he display during the act? Did Duncan awaken to see Macbeth kill him? All questions would lend greatly to an interpretation of Macbeth's character if answered, but the text does not grant its audience the luxury. What is known about the act however are two things; it did something to Macbeth's sanity and it was brutally violent.

Covered in blood and muttering vague and dark words, apart from his first and last soliloquies this is the most vulnerable Macbeth has been. It is clear he is shocked at the deed he has committed, and is potentially traumatised by the murder of his king and relative.

He is depicted in a state of paranoia, thinking he heard the voices of Duncan's servants as he committed the murder and forgetting to leave the daggers at the scene, putting him and his wife at great risk. Though it can be understood that Macbeth's guilt is one driven by his shame, with his line "I am to think what I have done... look on't again, I dare not" acting as strong evidence, his behaviour throughout this scene is more fitting of a man more afraid to be caught more than anything else.

Contextually, the murder Macbeth committed in this scene would have been the amongst the greatest crimes of not only Shakespeare's time but the real Macbeth's too. Though the real King Macbeth killed Duncan as well, it was on the field of battle and perceived as simply war. The plays version however was done deceitfully and as affront to God himself, for not only was killing one's family looked down upon, but the monarchy have always viewed their position as kings and queens as a holy right. By killing Duncan, Macbeth has committed a crime against God himself, and the consequences of such an action are dire. The fear Macbeth feels at such a revelation is displayed when telling his wife how he almost finished the prayer of Duncan's sleep-talking servants, almost exposing himself as Duncan's murderer and ruining his plans of ascension. As with many of the ideas presented by the play, Shakespeare does not make it clear if Macbeth is truly guilty of the murder or simply just afraid of being caught.

Further more, once again, it is Lady Macbeth who takes upon the role expected of a man, guarding her emotions and doing what is necessary to be done for the success of their plan. Though clearly still villainous, it is clear at this point that Shakespeare has designated Lady Macbeth as a strong and capable character, independent in her actions, and contrary to the gender standards of his time. It is also Lady Macbeth who introduces one of the many motifs found throughout the play: **blood and its association with guilt and eventually insanity.** By the end of the scene, her and her husband's hands are covered in the blood of Duncan, physically and metaphorically revealing their deed. Macbeth wonders if he can ever wash off the blood and by extension the murder he has committed, going so far to say that even the ocean itself cannot wash away his crime when he declares "with all great Neptune's ocean wash this blood? No... it will make the green turn red." Clearly feeling something associated with guilt, Macbeth appears in stark contrast to his wife, who states a "little water clears us of this deed" in an obvious biblical allusion to Pontius Pilate washing his hands after sentencing Christ to death. Shakespeare, however, cleverly uses this quote by Lady Macbeth and the guilt-ridden religious symbolism it references, and imbues it with dramatic irony, as **Lady Macbeth's madness towards the end of the play manifests itself with her paranoid desire to clean her hands of the phantom blood that only she can see.**

Act 2 Scene 3

Scene Summary

A porter early in the morning opens the castle gates for the thanes Macduff and Lennox. They question if they have come to early to escort Duncan from the castle, and upon seeing Macbeth approach, wonder if their knocking has awakened him. Macduff enters the king's bedchamber to greet and awaken him. Macbeth and Lennox discuss the troubled night, with Lennox specifically and eerily mentioning "strange screams of death."

Their conversation is interrupted by a screaming Macduff, revealing he has found the king dead, murdered in his bed. Lennox and Macbeth go to investigate while Macduff shouts for others to come, including Malcolm, Donalbain, and Banquo. His shouting wakes up Lady Macbeth, who confronts Macduff, demanding to know what is happening. Before Macduff can tell her, Banquo arrives, as Macduff informs both him and Lady Macbeth of what has occurred. She feigns shock, as Macbeth and Lennox arrive back from the chamber at the same time as Duncan's sons, Malcolm and Donalbain. Telling the princes what has happened, Lennox reveals he and Macbeth had found Duncan's servants holding daggers dripping with blood, and shocking everyone around him Macbeth reveals he killed both of the servants before they could speak. Questioning his motive, Macbeth assures Macduff that the killing of the servants was done in a fit of rage upon seeing Duncan, with his, "silver skin laced with golden blood." Lady Macbeth exits, feigning sickness, as Malcolm and Donalbain begin to have their own conversation, questioning why they haven't said anything in the presence of the lords. Before their conversation can continue, Banquo urges his fellow thanes to be brave as Macbeth calls for a meeting in the castle's hall. They all leave, except for Malcolm and Donalbain, who are uneasy in the presence of the thanes and suspect that their father's murderer may be targeting them. Donalbain agrees to travel to Ireland, while Malcolm is to flee to England, separating to ensure their safety.

Scene Analysis

Foil: a character designed to contrast with and emphasise the qualities of another character.

Whereas the previous scene dealt mainly with *Macbeth*'s emotional and supernatural themes, this one establishes much of the political conflict that will occur throughout the rest of the play. In doing so, it introduces another of *Macbeth*'s major characters, Macduff, whose role as Macbeth's **foil** is incredibly significant. Though minimal, the seeds of the rivalry are set, as unlike the other thanes within the play, Shakespeare writes Macduff with more significance – for instance, Macduff is the one to escort Duncan away from the castle, and discover Duncan's bloodied corpse, setting in motion the events that lead to Macbeth's ascension and downfall. From his horrified reaction to the death of King Duncan, the audience gathers that Macduff is incredibly loyal and is seeking order rather than chaos in the aftermath of Duncan's death, summoning as many people as he can to tell them of the king's death. Macbeth, as the audience would expect knowing he committed the murder, is written showing the opposite behaviour, trying to create as much disorder as possible to shift suspicion. Macbeth's killing of the servants is a deliberate and suspicious action, and to the audience is amongst the first indicators that a very different Macbeth has emerged in the wake of murdering Duncan – one devoid of the hesitation and fear seen previously.

Aside from introducing Macduff as a foil, this scene serves to introduce another literary idea: **hidden information,** and the notion that all is not what it seems. The deliberate decision to not show Duncan's murder is highly contrasted here, as the audience is made witness to the shocking and chaotic fallout of the death of a king. Macduff's shouts of "O horror, horror, horror," Macbeth's admittance to killing the supposed murderers, and Lady Macbeth's either real or feigned fainting episode all create an atmosphere of stress and high drama. Cleverly, Shakespeare (much like Macbeth shifting attention elsewhere in order to hide his wrong doing) deliberately shifts the attention of his audience in order to hide hidden truths and motifs. Yet ironically, the audience already knows all there is to know but cannot warn or notify the characters of Macbeth's wrongdoing. Thus, characters like Donalbain and specifically Malcolm, like the audience at the beginning of the play, begin to suspect that all is not as it seems. Their private conversation amongst the middle of the shouting in reaction of Duncan's death indicate strong wills and caution, with their mutual decision to flee rather than remain to investigate ultimately saving their lives. Compared to Banquo who decides to flee too late and ends up killed, Malcolm and Donalbain's flight set them up as formidable forces against Macbeth's reign, and to the audience add a sense of tension, for up until this point, Lady Macbeth's sharp wit and scheming seemed unmatched by anyone.

Act 2 Scene 4

Scene Summary

Some time after the previous scene, the thane Ross talks with an old man about the strange occurrences in nature after Duncan's murder, including a falcon killed by an owl and Duncan's horses going mad and gruesomely eating each other in their stables. Macduff enters and they ask him for any important news. Macduff tells them it is believed that Duncan's servants were the ones who killed the king, mentioning that Macbeth had killed them, while Malcolm and Donalbain have fled Scotland, marking them as suspects in the murder. Ross thinks the crown shall be granted to Macbeth, to which Macduff replies that Macbeth has already travelled to be crowned, while Duncan is to be buried with his ancestors. Ross questions if Macduff will attend Macbeth's coronation but Macduff responds that he is heading home instead. Bidding them goodbye, the men disperse as the act ends.

Scene Analysis

As the final scene of the act, much like many of the shorter scenes that have come before, this serves more of a reminder of events that have happened, and foreshadows what is to come. Once again, Shakespeare uses the motif of **supernatural disorder plaguing Scotland.** This time, much like Duncan's death, incidents occur off-stage, adding to the eerie atmosphere of the play, and heralding Macbeth's dark reign as king, for in the same scene in which the audience hears that Duncan's horses have eaten each other, they find out alongside Macduff that Macbeth is travelling to be crowned. Shakespeare's weaving of motifs, symbolism, and foreshadowing is incredibly effective in setting up the tragic action to come.

This is also the scene in which Macduff's suspicions of Macbeth are first hinted at, as when asked if he is going to travel to attend Macbeth's coronation, he says he is not, and notes he is riding home. Though on an explicit level such an action is seemingly innocent of suspicious intent, upon closer inspection of Macduff's character (especially considering his loyalty to the crown displayed in the previous scene), it is telling that the same dedication shown to Duncan as king is not shifted to Macbeth. Macduff is not blindly loyal to whoever happens to be the king (especially under suspicious circumstances!) – he is loyal to the *rightful* king, hence his eventual allegiance with Malcolm.

Act 3 Scene 1
Scene Summary

This act opens with Banquo alone, preparing to depart. He contemplates Macbeth's rise to power and how it matches the witches' prophecy, though he suspects it was done using unworthy means. Hushing himself hearing people approach, Banquo realises Macbeth and Lady Macbeth enter, now king and queen of Scotland, along with their servants and thanes. They greet Banquo kindly and ask if he is to stay for the feast. He refuses, saying he is going for a ride, but will return by nightfall. Macbeth remarks that his advice would have been helpful at a council discussing his nephews Malcolm and Donalbain, who he claims have confessed to murdering Duncan, though the audience knows this to be a lie. After asking if Fleance, Banquo's son, is riding with him, Macbeth allows Banquo to leave, wishing him luck on his ride. After he leaves, Macbeth asks a servant to bring the men waiting for him outside the castle. Left alone, Macbeth wonders about the threat that Banquo presents to his rule, fearful of his noble nature and the wisdom he possesses. He worries about the witches' prophecy to him, and remembers how Banquo laughed when the witches first pronounced Macbeth as king, before asking them himself and being told he will produce a line of kings. He fears that someone outside his family will snatch the kingship, and grows angry, declaring he will make his own future and do what needs to be done.

He then welcomes two murderers into his presence, asking them if they thought on what he had told them the day before when they first met. He tells them it was Banquo who made their lives miserable, not him, and asks if they're simply going to let Banquo go unpunished for keeping their families in poverty. They respond simply that they're men, but Macbeth compares them to lowly dogs, provoking them by stating that by killing Banquo they can climb higher towards Macbeth's position. By capitalising on their anger at the world, Macbeth manipulates them into seeing Banquo as their enemy. Macbeth claims he would kill Banquo himself if it wasn't for their common allies, and once receiving the support of the murderers, orders them to wait on the road and to kill Banquo and Fleance. Ordering them to leave, much like before he killed Duncan, Macbeth states ominously that "Banquo thy soul's flight. / If it find heaven, must find it out tonight."

Scene Analysis

Jumping forward in time, this scene serves to establish the consequences of Duncan's death and the new world Scotland finds itself in under Macbeth's rule. Banquo mirrors the audience once again, as much like the opening of Act 2, he voices his unease and suspicion at Macbeth's sudden ascension and more importantly, his seeming fulfilment of the prophecy. Initially, Shakespeare sets a scene of almost normalcy, with Macbeth and Lady Macbeth appearing as gracious and kind hosts, yet the idea of the **seen and unseen** arises again, with Banquo's previous confession of unease and the secret plot to kill Banquo started by Macbeth. Macbeth's hiring of the murderers is a curious action at first glance, as up until this point in the play, all the deaths required to see him in power had two things in common: they were planned by Lady Macbeth and carried out by Macbeth's own hand. To start with the first point, Lady Macbeth's absence from this plan and the majority of this act is a subtle hint of her diminished role as the play continues, for in the next scene we see a shift in her character's personality and actions. Instead, it is Macbeth who plots and manipulates the murders, once again defying his contextual gender role, as instead of going and killing Banquo and Fleance himself, he hires murderers to do the work for him and manipulates them into blaming Banquo for all their problems.

The murderers themselves are curious, as the way Shakespeare writes their dialogue full of lines such as "the vile blows and buffers of the world hath incensed me that I spite the world" possibly hint that the murderers are not professional assassins but rather disgruntled common folk. Shakespeare includes an analogy spoken by Macbeth in reference to dogs and how each dog has role in the world: "the valued file," as Macbeth puts it. This could be interpreted as Shakespeare making a political statement about the unjust nature of the feudal system, but considering Macbeth is wrongful shifting blame to Banquo, it becomes clearer that Shakespeare is highlighting the **wrongful use of power and the damaging effects it can have on others.** Aside from themes of power, the issue of destiny once again arises, as before meeting the murderers, Macbeth contemplates the witches' prophecy again. He is aware enough to recognise that the prophecy of his kingship included no line about an heir of his, but the audience is left to question why Macbeth would even want to take power if he would leave no legacy behind. The answer lies in the famous quote "absolute power corrupts absolutely" – Shakespeare presents Macbeth as a changed man compared to how he was in the first two acts, hiring murderers instead of doing killing by his own hand.

Act 3 Scene 2
Scene Summary

Within the castle, Lady Macbeth questions a servant if Banquo has left yet, and she learns that he has. Ordering them to bring Macbeth to her, she contemplates whether it is worth getting what you desire while wracked with anxiety because of it. Macbeth enters, and Lady Macbeth asks why he is always alone with thoughts of dead men long buried. Macbeth claims he would rather be dead than be consumed by the endless nightmares plaguing him, saying at least the men he killed are at peace. He thinks of Duncan, and how nothing can hurt him anymore because they had hurt him so much by betraying him in life.

Lady Macbeth comforts her husband, asking him to relax and appear happy amongst his guests tonight. He agrees and asks her to treat Banquo with extra care tonight, as he is their biggest threat at the moment. Frustrated, she asks him to stop speaking that way, but he claims his mind is "full of scorpions" while Banquo and Fleance still live. She comforts him once again saying they can't live forever, to which Macbeth responds in agreement, remarking that before nightfall, something dreadful is to be done. When asking what he has planned, he stops her, stating it would be better for it to be done successfully before he tells her what it is. He turns to the night sky and calls for it to "tear that great bond which keeps me pale" before asking his wife to walk with him to the feast.

Scene Analysis

This is another intimate scene between Macbeth and Lady Macbeth, revealing much about the journeys their respective characters are to take, contributing to the theme of guilt prevalent throughout the play. Macbeth's troubled mind returns from Act 2 as he struggles to feel comfortable in his position of power. Though Shakespeare has granted him such a position within the plot, he allows Macbeth to feel vulnerable and unsure of his position. Contextually, Macbeth (being a male in a **patriarchal** society) should feel comfortable in his position and poised to take rule. Yet Macbeth is a much more complex character than the **archetypal** king, and displays a confusing mix of guilt and paranoia within this scene. His quote of **"full of scorpions is my mind"** seemingly indicates to the audience that he feels guilty about some of his actions and the 'stinging' memories of such wrongdoing plagues his sleep. The **motif of sleep** within the play is prominent; the admission of not being able to comfortably rest is an implicit sign of guilt, as in the final act Lady Macbeth is shown to sleepwalk and vaguely admit her crimes. The honesty of such guilt is something audiences may still question, however; is Macbeth truly guilty and remorseful, or paranoid about being found out? In the context of this scene, it appears to be more of the latter, as though Lady Macbeth specifically mentions Duncan, it appears Macbeth is troubled by Banquo, Fleance, and their respective connections to the witches' initial prophecy.

> **Patriarchy:** a society where men are dominant.
>
> **Archetypal:** a perfectly typical example of something.

He specifically tells her that it is Banquo whom he considers a "scorpion." If we assume a belief in the supernatural, as Macbeth does, it is clear why Banquo is a threat, as if all the witches told was true, then Macbeth would leave no heir to continue his line of kings. Though unjust in his actions, Macbeth's paranoia is justifiable but ironically it is **his wife's soothing words that shift his paranoia into pure obsession.**

Throughout the play up until this point, Lady Macbeth has been portrayed as the text's pure villain, encouraging and manipulating Macbeth to murder Duncan. She went as far to shame him and defy her role of a noble lady to see such goals completed.

Yet throughout the third act, with only a small moment in the next scene, she is softer with Macbeth and rather than manipulate her husband, she comforts him, a role expected of a noble woman. This shift in her character is interesting as while she reverts to a position of passivity and comfort, Macbeth rises to one of action and darkness. Her soothing line of "But in them nature's copy isn't eternal," referencing that Banquo and Fleance cannot live forever, seems to give Macbeth confidence in his plot to murder them. In a dark reflection of earlier scenes, it is now Macbeth who actively schemes to advance his position while his wife remains in the dark.

Act 3 Scene 3

Scene Summary

In the middle of the night, the three murderers lie in wait for Banquo. They question the third, asking him who sent him. After telling them it was Macbeth, they trust him and discuss the setting sun, meaning Banquo is nearby. As they wait, they hear Banquo call for a torch, and spot him riding with his son Fleance. They attack, killing Banquo, but extinguish the torch and allow Fleance to escape. Disappointed that they lost Fleance, the murderers decide to return to Macbeth to tell him what they achieved.

Scene Analysis

Though not a large scene, the death of Banquo is a highly important point in the play as it not only reveals much about what Macbeth's character has become but has implications for the rest of the plot. Banquo, while not the most prominent character, was one who held great importance to the overall story, as aside from Macbeth, he was the only person to witness the witches and receive a prophecy himself.

Whether a victim of circumstance or not, Banquo's role on a wider literary level was almost like a mirror to Macbeth. Not quite on the level of a foil like Macduff, Banquo was more of a reflection of Macbeth, taking the opposite approach to receiving a life-changing prophecy. Whereas Macbeth went down a path of greed, ambition, and eventually evil to **manifest** his destiny, Banquo showed no desire to claim the throne to ensure his heirs become kings; rather, he remained loyal to the crown, and even became suspicious of Macbeth's rise to power after Duncan's death.

Manifest: to demonstrate or bring something about.

Banquo is what Macbeth could have been without his fatal flaw of ambition and the presence of his scheming wife, and his death acts as a reminder of how far Macbeth has truly fallen. At least with the death of Duncan, Shakespeare had Macbeth do the deed himself, granting some twisted form of honour on his behalf considering the medieval Scottish context. Banquo, however, was killed by common murderers, underscoring to the audience how little honour Macbeth truly has left if he must resort to hiring killers rather than facing and killing Banquo and his son himself.

One important note for this scene is that Fleance escapes, and while this is not hugely important for the play, Fleance was supposedly the ancestor to King James I of England, Shakespeare's royal patron at the time of *Macbeth*'s release. His survival not only keeps intact the idea that destiny cannot be changed, but was an important political decision for Shakespeare to keep favour with royalty.

Act 3 Scene 4

Scene Summary

The scene opens with a banquet set for the various thanes, with Macbeth and Lady Macbeth presiding. Macbeth greets his guests and welcomes them to the feast before one of the murderers approaches him. The murderer tells Macbeth that the blood he is covered in is from slitting Banquo's throat. Pleased, Macbeth praises him before asking if Fleance has been killed alongside his father. When he tells him that Fleance escaped, Macbeth admits he is afraid once more as his perfect plan has been ruined, and enquires if Banquo is truly dead. The murderer assures him that Banquo is "safe in a ditch... with twenty trenched gashes in his head." Though still unsettled by Fleance's escape, Macbeth calms himself stating at this point Fleance is no threat. Dismissing the murderer, Lady Macbeth approaches and asks Macbeth to stop being anti-social so that his thanes do not become alienated from him. While Macbeth is distracted giving a toast to the thanes, the ghost of Banquo enters and sits in Macbeth's seat in the hall. When announcing he hoped Banquo was late out of rudeness, the thanes invite him to sit amongst them, gesturing to what they see as an empty seat. Macbeth, however, sees the bloodied ghost of Banquo.

He shouts and demands who planned for Banquo's ghost to appear, and the thanes are confused as to what is happening, as Macbeth yells "thou canst not say I did it... never shake thy gory locks at me!" Ross calls for the thanes to rise, stating the king is not well, but Lady Macbeth runs to stop them claiming Macbeth is suffering from a minor condition he has had since childhood, promising them that it is only a temporary fit. Turning to her husband, she furiously asks if he is a man, to which he responds he is if he can stare at such a horrific sight. She admonishes him, saying it is the same imaginary visions as the phantom dagger that lead him to Duncan, telling him it doesn't even seem like real fear but more like a woman telling a scary story around a fire. She shames him saying he is making such horrific faces at an empty stool. Macbeth begs her to look at the stool and questions the ghost's purpose if it cannot speak or act. It vanishes, and Lady Macbeth questions what has caused such a reaction, disbelieving him when he tells her it was Banquo. He ominously states much that blood has been spilt in the past, but when the ancient dead were killed, they stayed dead but "now they rise again... and push us from our stools."

She reminds him that he has ignored his thanes and Macbeth apologises for his behaviour stating it was due to a strange condition. Macbeth toasts Banquo, and the ghost appears again, making Macbeth shout at the ghost to go away or appear as some fearsome beast instead of a murdered Banquo.

The ghost disappears once again, the thanes ask what Macbeth has seen, but before he can answer, Lady Macbeth states he is unwell and asking questions will lead to further trouble. She apologises and dismisses the banquet quickly, before turning to her husband. He tells her that **"blood will have blood"** and states he will send spies to find Macduff, before revealing he is to visit the witches the next day. She asks if he has slept, and he finally agrees to return to bed.

Scene Analysis

Macbeth's encounter with Banquo's ghost is a crucial turning point in the play, both thematically and plot-wise. There is so much symbolism, thematic meaning, and foreshadowing within this single encounter that this entire scene analysis will be dedicated to unravelling it all! First and foremost is the question of whether the ghost is even real, or a figment of Macbeth's guilt-ridden and paranoid mind.

Throughout the play, Shakespeare has deliberately utilised supernatural elements and indicated that magic is a true force within the text's world, though much of what relates to Macbeth is left vague. Macbeth is given a prophecy but it could be argued that due to the **ambiguous** wording and nature of it, Macbeth's fate might have followed the same **trajectory** without the magical prophecy, as Macbeth was made Thane of Cawdor before his encounter with the witches. Using this logic, the ghost of Banquo, much like the dagger that lead Macbeth to Duncan, appears to be a simple figment of Macbeth's broken mind, with even Lady Macbeth pointing out as such when she remarks "this is the very painting of your fear... the air drawn dagger," though ironically Lady Macbeth will soon experience her own guilt-ridden hallucinations. Contextual evidence also supports this, as Scotland during the 11th century was a very superstitious place, with undead spirits being perceived as works of evil and omens of darkness. Macbeth would have great knowledge of such superstition, and displays it when he ominously warns "blood will have blood" in relation to the vengeance undead spirits were believed to have possessed against those who wronged them in life. It must also be stated that Macbeth's lack of sleep is another powerful indicator of the ghost not being real, as sleep deprivation is known to cause visual hallucinations. Yet it must be stated that this perception of events is from a modern and scientific perspective, a perspective that Shakespeare's highly superstitious 17th century audience lacked, so on an explicit level, we can argue the reality of Banquo's ghost either way.

Ambiguous: open to interpretation; not having one obvious meaning.

Trajectory: the journey that a character undergoes.

Guilt is the most obvious of theme in this scene. Though it has come up over and over again when analysing Macbeth's various visions and monologues, this time is different. For one, Macbeth's reaction is not one of thoughtfulness or even the softer, subtler fear shown in the aftermath of Duncan's death, but an example of pure terror. Shakespeare has written Macbeth in this scene as if he is going mad, ranting and raving at what seems to be nothing to those around him. This shift is likely due to Macbeth being granted a physical reminder of his wrongdoing and the consequences of his search for power. The fact that Shakespeare wrote the ghost to simply sit and stare at Macbeth also adds great weight and unease. It is a clever literary trick to intensify its dark meaning. Leaving the message unspoken allows for his audience to interpret the true nature of Macbeth's guilt and what it means for his character going forward. The theme of guilt is further supported by the motif of blood again, as much like Macbeth wondering if he can wash the blood of Duncan off his hands, here Macbeth is confronted with two figures covered in Banquo's blood: the murderer and the ghost. It is important to note that every scene blood has appeared in so far has delved into the consequences of Macbeth's actions and what it means for his future, and as in this scene, though it is eventually resolved, the unnerving display and nature of his words sow suspicion amongst his subjects – suspicion that eventually leads to their rebellion.

Briefly, it should be noted that in Shakespeare's tragic act formula, this scene serves as the **first climax** of the play. The first climax, almost always in the middle of Act 3, is an event that shapes the future of the play to come and is usually the peak and release of the tension built up until that point. In the case of *Macbeth*, the first climax comes at a point at which all the spiritual, political, and emotional tension built up by Macbeth's actions have finally come to a head, with Macbeth finally confronted by the consequences of his actions. It is a powerful moment and one that influences the protagonists of the play to begin their plan that will eventually lead to their fall. For Macbeth, the plan includes his second visit to the witches and sudden knowledge of Macduff's flight, both leading to one his most horrific actions of the play: murdering Macduff's family.

Act 3 Scene 5

Scene Summary

Somewhere unknown, the three witches once again meet in the middle of a storm, this time with their master **Hecate, goddess of the moon and magic.** They ask why Hecate is angry with them. She tells them they had no right to consort with Macbeth and grant him prophecies without her presence and knowledge. She reminds them she is the source of their power and they have done all this for a man who is "spiteful and wrathful" who "loves his own ends, not for you." Hecate says they can make amends however, and orders them to meet her again soon, as Macbeth will soon seek their wisdom once more to know his destiny. She tells them to prepare their spells and cauldrons, as she is planning something dark, stating Macbeth will "spurn fate, scorn death... think he is above wisdom, grace and fear." Hecate then disappears as the witches hurry to do her bidding.

Scene Analysis

Aside from the ghost of Banquo, the presence of Hecate throughout the play is amongst its most overtly supernatural elements. Traditionally a Greek goddess, Hecate is here portrayed as a representation of the fearsome and unknown nature of magic in the play's world. Mentioned only by name previously, much like Macbeth at the beginning of the text, Hecate already has a well-established presence with her name mentioned when characters talk of dark forces, such as Macbeth in Act 2 Scene 2, stating "witchcraft celebrates pale Hecate's offerings" before murdering Duncan. It is made clear early on that Hecate is an immensely terrifying and powerful being, and that fact is further established here as even the witches tremble before her presence. This is important, as up until this point, the witches have been portrayed as incredibly powerful beings capable of predicting the future and vanishing into thin air. With the introduction of Hecate, Shakespeare almost creates an atmosphere of **existential dread,** as her simple presence and command over the witches conveys to the audience that the squabbles of man seem insignificant before her judgement. Hence, Hecate can be interpreted as Shakespeare's **physical representation of the theme of destiny.** As she states in the scene, she is there to punish Macbeth for thinking he is the master of his destiny and above what she quotes as "wisdom, grace and fear." On a literary and symbolic level, Hecate promotes the idea that one should not meddle with magic forces above their understanding, especially their destiny, for dark things come to those who do. Though not explicitly causing Macbeth's downfall, Hecate perfectly highlights and **manipulates the fatal flaw of ambition,** as she knows he is not just seeking to claim the crown any more but is **ambitious enough to attempt to become the master of his fate.** This is why she instructs her witches to show him more visions, as ironically, she knows no matter their vague meaning, they will eventually lead to his demise, acting as obvious foreshadowing for the audience.

> **Existential dread:** feeling uneasy about mortality and the meaning of life.

Her presence, it should also be noted, is another example of Shakespeare using context to increase the tension and drama of the play, as to his highly religious audience, the use of a **pagan** goddess who is portrayed as the master of the witches, is a powerful and dark image that would inspire great fear amongst them, building the play's dark and oppressive atmosphere. Finally, on the topic of Hecate, it appears once again that Shakespeare has employed another strong female presence, this time one who wields **immense, unforeseen power.** Yet much like the witches and Lady Macbeth, this is done in a somewhat negative light unfortunately, as her association with the witches and being a pagan goddess would invite great fear and loathing from the audience, with many assuming she is the true villain of the play as it is hinted that she is the one responsible for the prophecies and fate of Macbeth.

> **Pagan:** polytheistic religions that differ from the three major world religions (Christianity, Islam, and Judaism).

Act 3 Scene 6

Scene Summary

This scene begins with the thane Lennox meeting another unnamed lord. He speaks to the lord about the mysterious events currently occurring in Scotland, including the deaths of Duncan and Banquo. He suggests that Fleance may have killed his father, much like Malcolm and Donalbain were suspected to have killed Duncan. In a sarcastic tone, he praises Macbeth for killing Duncan's two servants while drunk and asleep, stating it was "nobly done? Ay and wisely too." He declares that Malcolm and Donalbain are better off not being captured by Macbeth before inquiring about Macduff, who he claims is living in disgrace. The lord responds that he is with Malcolm, who has found himself in the English court, and is expected by King Edward. He reveals that Macduff has joined with Malcolm to aid him in forming an alliance with Siward, the Lord of Northumberland. Macduff, he explains, wishes to bring peace and prosperity back to Scotland, free from Macbeth's **tyranny**. Hearing the news that Macduff has betrayed him, Macbeth is preparing for war. The lord continues, stating that Macbeth sent a messenger to retrieve Macduff back to Scotland but was refused. Lennox seems pleased with the news, saying it would be good for a messenger to tell Macduff to return swiftly to free Scotland from oppression.

> **Tyranny:** cruel, oppressive, despotic government or rule.

Scene Analysis

This scene at first appears confusing, as the words spoken and tone seem to shift from supporting Macbeth to actively plotting against him. However, this makes a lot more sense when we realise this scene is highly sarcastic! Lennox is one of the more prominent thanes, as throughout the play, he and Ross seem to have the most dialogue and influence over events. This is important to note, as by using a character as established as Lennox to be the first direct voice against Macbeth, **Shakespeare gives weight to the rebellion.** When analysing Lennox's lines about "noble Macbeth" slaying Duncan's two servants before they could commit their crime and men being careful about walking out too late, it becomes clear he is mocking Macbeth and beginning to see his true nature as king. The previous scene with Hecate demonstrated the spiritual foreshadowing of Macbeth's downfall, but this scene is the opposite, showing the **political fallout of Macbeth's tyranny.** The mention of Macduff fleeing to England and Malcolm's alliance with Siward all foreshadow the war to come, and truly highlight the terrible position Macbeth has put himself in. Shakespeare is seemingly trying to punish Macbeth's **hubris** as much as possible, **as both his spiritual and political worlds begin to collapse in on him.** With the knowledge that Macbeth is going to visit the witches again and Macduff's defiance learned from Lennox, Shakespeare establishes and foreshadows the play's dramatic and tragic climax, with Macbeth's second set of prophecies, the annihilation of Macduff's family, and the war for the Scottish throne to come!

> **Hubris:** excessive pride; self-confidence.

Act 4 Scene 1

Scene Summary

In an unknown place, the three witches once again meet as they gather around a cauldron. Mixing a grotesque potion, they all chant dark words, "Double, double toil and trouble / Fire burn and cauldron bubble" while they work, eventually summoning their master, the goddess Hecate, who leaves as quick as she came. Sensing "something wicked this way comes," the witches greet Macbeth, who questions what the witches' power truly does. They tell him it is a "deed without a name," and Macbeth, much like at the beginning of the play, demands for them to answer his questions. They offer to Macbeth a chance to talk to their "masters," as three apparitions appear in turn before him. The first is an armoured head, who when Macbeth asks for its wisdom, tells him to **beware of Macduff.** A second apparition appears, this time in the form of a bloody child. The child tells him that **no man born of a woman can ever harm him** before disappearing. Macbeth arrogantly uses this second revelation to dismiss the first prophecy of Macduff killing him before the third apparition appears – a crowned child holding a tree in his hand. The last apparition tells him no harm shall come to Macbeth until, **"Great Birnam Wood to high Dunsinane hill shall come against him."**

Content by what he has heard, he demands the prophecies he was given come true, lest the witches be cursed. Before he can leave, however, the witches grant him one final horrific vision. Eight kings, with the last holding a mirror and Banquo's ghost appearing before Macbeth, mutilated and gross, frightening him. He orders them gone as they vanish before his eyes and demands to know from the witches what he just witnessed. They laugh and ask each other why Macbeth isn't happy before dancing and vanishing once again as music begins to play from nowhere. The thane Lennox enters and asks what is wrong. Macbeth asks if he had seen the witches, to which Lennox replies no, but he brings news of a rider who bore the message that Macduff had fled to England. Speaking to himself, Macbeth makes the decision to stop hesitating and act upon his ambition. He resolves to raid Macduff's lands of Fife, destroying his castle and killing his wife and children immediately less he forget his purpose, and promises to seek no more visions. Speaking to Lennox once more he orders him to take him to the messengers.

Scene Analysis

Macbeth's second meeting with the witches is not only one the most important scene of Act 4, but is also amongst the most significant overall when considering its impact on the play's climax. Before breaking down Macbeth's visions and what they mean thematically, we should analyse this scene's role and placement in Shakespeare's tragic formula. Act 4 in Shakespearean tragedies is usually reserved for the calm that comes after the storm of events that is Act 3, and such calm allows for the characters to gain knowledge and formulate plans that will influence events to come in Act 5. In the case of *Macbeth*, Act 4 contains three separate perspectives for the three scenes, with each ultimately setting up the conflict between Macbeth and Malcolm, and Macduff's prophetic role in the fall of Macbeth.

Concerning this scene specifically, Macbeth's second set of visions heavily foreshadow what lies in Macbeth's future, including his end, and influence Macbeth's character in such a major way, as he undergoes a fearsome and dark transformation. It should also be mentioned that this is the final scene in which the witches appear within the play, or any blatant supernatural forces for that matter, as from this point on, the play is dedicated to the human struggle between its characters.

The interpretation of the true meaning of the prophecies is the logical next step in this analysis, but their overall meaning and fulfilment is made very clear by the play's end. Instead, analysing how each prophecy reflects and influences the themes of *Macbeth* and the titular character himself would be more beneficial. To begin, the first prophecy given by the vision of an armoured head, telling him to "beware Macduff" is blatant foreshadowing of the nature of Macbeth's death at the hands of Macduff, as in the final scene Macduff gives Malcolm the bloody head of Macbeth, slain in battle. The meaning of the head aside, the warning given to Macbeth about Macduff feeds his paranoia and ambition to hold his power, causing him to quote "to crown my thoughts with acts, be it thought and done," beginning the path of willingly acting upon every thought without consideration of consequence. However, this mindset is incredibly self-destructive as the consequences of his actions against Macduff specifically lead to Macduff's fury against him and the eventual fulfilment of the second prophecy: the image of a bloody child quoting "none of woman born shall harm Macbeth," which symbolically foreshadows Macduff's role in Act 5. The bloody child can be interpreted as Macduff, taken from his mother's womb as a caesarean birth, connoting the violent destiny Macduff holds in relation to Macbeth. Once again, the themes of violence and destiny are interwoven within this scene, as on a grand scale it was almost as if **Macduff was born to end the cycle of violence Macbeth has inflicted upon Scotland.**

These are powerful ideas, and having them raised in a supernatural context to a highly superstitious audience would have created immense tension and drama when viewed. When considering the weight granted by the previous two prophecies, the third almost seems laughable in comparison, as a young boy holding the branch of a tree quoting, "Macbeth shall never be vanquished until Great Birnam Wood to high Dunsinane hill shall come against him" does not seem to mesh with the other two prophecies other than confirm Macbeth's seeming invincibility. Macbeth dismisses it as such, stating "that will never be: Who can impress the forest, bid the tree unfix his earthbound root?"

Macbeth's hubris and growing arrogance has been steadily growing throughout the play, but it is the introduction and blatant dismissal of the third prophecy that truly highlights this to the audience. Though seemingly ridiculous, the concept of Birnam Wood moving to Dunsinane castle in a world of witches and prophecy isn't completely impossible. The way Shakespeare interprets the prophecy is incredibly clever, using it to subtly undermine Macbeth's confidence of his own invincibility. On a basic level, Macbeth's dismissal of this prophecy and the one before goes against his belief that prophecies are absolute. Instead, he acts erratically, believing he is immortal and the master of his own destiny.

Shakespeare throughout the play has made clear that when coming into contact with the supernatural, **expectations are made to be broken.** Destiny throughout the entire play so far has been highlighted as an incredibly powerful thing, and Macbeth thinking he is above it is a clear sign of his tragic downfall to come. The witches themselves even attempt to reign in Macbeth's ambition, telling him to "seek no more." Yet, thinking he is above even them, he ignores their warning and asks if Banquo's heirs will ever rule Scotland. Shakespeare then writes that the witches create a vision showing ten ghostly kings and Banquo, seemingly striking fear into the heart of Macbeth. Through the imagery of them holding sceptres and crowns, it is implied that these are the heirs of Banquo and the true kings of Scotland after Macbeth. This vision is a clear warning of Macbeth's mortality and the absolute nature of prophecy, even those as ridiculous as the Birnam Wood one, and if Macbeth were not so blinded by his ambition would take measures in order to avoid or at least **mitigate** the tragic and violent fate that awaits him.

Mitigate: to alleviate or reduce the severity of something.

Act 4 Scene 2

Scene Summary

Shifting to the setting of Macduff's castle in Fife, the scene opens with the introduction of Lady Macduff talking with the thane Ross. Lady Macduff asks Ross why her husband has fled their lands, and he tells her to be patient. She admonishes her husband for having no patience himself and deems his flight as madness, for now she worries her family are branded as traitors. Ross counters this, telling her she does not know if it was wisdom or fear that made him flee, to which she responds scathingly: "wisdom? To leave his wife, to leave his babies, his mansion and his titles in a place from whence himself does fly?" She **castigates** him for lacking the courage to defend his family, and believes he has left out of fear. Ross tries to calm her, reassuring her that her husband is noble and wise and does what is required of him.

Castigate: severely reprimand or admonish someone for doing something wrong.

He tells her its not safe to discuss such things when people can be accused of treason without trial or reason. He tells her he will return as soon as he can. Alone with her son, she boldly tells him his father is dead, but her son refuses to believe it, seemingly far more hopeful about their future than his mother. She despairingly asks what he is to do without a father, to which he boldly counters by asking what she is to do without a husband. When her son asks if his father was a traitor, she says yes. Discussing what a traitor is and who should bring justice to those who break oaths, the two interrupted by a messenger. The messenger tells Lady Macduff that great danger approaches and that she must leave with her children lest they be killed, but as soon as the messenger leaves, the murderers arrive. They ask where Macduff is, and she bravely tells them she hopes he is far beyond their reach. Her son defends Macduff's reputation, shouting that he isn't a traitor which prompts the murderers to kill him. Lady Macduff then shouts and runs as she is pursued by the murderers, and is killed.

Scene Analysis

This is one of the rare scenes away from Macbeth's perspective, though his shadow looms dark over this horrific sequences of events. Before analysing the major theme of this scene, a quick look at the brief and tragic character of Lady Macduff is necessary. In contrast to the witches and Lady Macbeth, Shakespeare presents Lady Macduff in the role expected by her context. Running Macduff's castle and raising their children, Lady Macduff easily embodies the typical medieval noble woman of her time. At no point is she scheming or seen to possess any supernatural powers, and from what can be gleaned from this brief scene, she is a decent and caring woman, concerned about her family's safety in the wake of Macduff's flight from Scotland. Yet even though Lady Macduff is delegated such a traditional role throughout the story, Shakespeare still grants her a degree of strength and prominence. Her first line of "what had he done, to make him fly the land" immediately displays to the audience the independence of her character, as she demands answers concerning her husband's whereabouts and reason for leaving. Not once holding back her opinion, Lady Macduff almost seems like the female foil for Lady Macbeth, as her blunt, honest, and maternal nature is the opposite of the scheming, manipulative and arguably **androgynous** personality Lady Macbeth has shown throughout the play. By introducing a character as seemingly good and strong as Lady Macduff, only to have her and entire family killed in the same scene was a bold decision by Shakespeare. The level of violence to have a child killed on-stage is confronting by even today's standards, truly highlighting the harrowing nature of violence Shakespeare has attempted to convey to his audience.

Androgynous: having characteristics of both male and female sexes.

The slaughter of Macduff's family, for the simple reason that he journeys to speak to Malcolm, is a clear sign that **Macbeth has truly turned to darkness and is now the play's primary antagonist.** From wavering against killing Duncan, to without hesitation ordering the murder of an entire family, the consequences of Macbeth's unrelenting ambition for power and security of his rule are brutally displayed here. In the next scene, Macduff wavers somewhat in supporting Malcolm's rebellion, but these uncertainties are quashed when Macduff learns that Macbeth has killed his family. Thus, Macbeth's actions create a powerful political enemy capable of destroying him. The consequences for Macduff are especially heartbreaking, as him choosing loyalty to his country over his family led to their deaths. The grief caused by such an action is felt by all, as even before they're murdered, Lady Macduff tells her son that "your father is dead" to convey the seeming abandonment he has inflicted. This lends a great deal of depth to Macduff's character, and makes his decisions in the next scene all the more compelling.

Act 4 Scene 3

Scene Summary

This scene begins with Macduff and Malcolm looking for a place to talk. Malcolm admits he wishes to weep for the death of his father and the consequences for the country, but Macduff tells him to hold strong in the face of Macbeth's tyranny. Malcolm declares he will do what is right and avenge what he thinks is worthy to be avenged, and talks of how Macbeth was once an honourable man who held Macduff in high honour. He questions if Macduff would betray him to Macbeth. Macduff declares he is no traitor, but Malcolm counters that a king's command can sway even the most loyal men. Malcolm worries that if he topples Macbeth, a worse king will rise in his place, as "all the particulars of vice so grafted... that when they shall be opened black Macbeth will seem as pure as snow." Macduff counters that you couldn't find anyone worse than Macbeth, to which Malcolm agrees stating no one can be as "false, deceitful and malicious" as Macbeth, but the two men are dancing around the topic of open rebellion – both Malcolm and Macduff think Macbeth is unfit to be king, but both of them are hesitant to announce their disloyalty.

Malcolm then lays a trap to test whether Macduff truly has Scotland's best interests at heart. Malcolm pretends to confess that he is exceedingly lustful, but Macduff reassures him to not be afraid to take what is his by right and that they can hide Malcolm's secret desires while still ensuring he appears virtuous. Malcolm then admits to greed, stating if he becomes king he will "cut off the nobles for their lands and jewels." Macduff is a little more shaken, noting that greed is the downfall of kings and a worse vice than lust, but tells Malcolm that if he becomes king of Scotland such greed can be satisfied. Malcolm still refuses, claiming he doesn't have any of the qualities of being a good king, which to him include "justice, temperance, mercy, patience, courage and lowliness." Macduff angrily declares that Malcolm is not fit to be king and that this knowledge has destroyed all hope for Macduff to ever return to the precious Scotland he loves. He admonishes Malcolm, telling him his father Duncan was a virtuous king and his mother spent nearly her whole life in prayer.

Surprised by the strength of Macduff's outburst, **Malcolm finally believes Macduff's loyalty** and reveals all the ill things he said about himself before are not true – in fact, Malcolm is so virtuous that the only lies he has told in his entire life were the words he just told Macduff. He agrees to free Scotland from Macbeth's tyranny with an army lead by the English earl Siward. Macduff (who has a bit of emotional whiplash at this point!) then discusses his hopes for healing the land. Ross then enters and informs them that Scotland is indeed a "poor country... where sighs and groans and shrieks rend the air." Malcolm confirms that he will return with an army, and Ross wishes he could be happy but explains that he carries dark news for Macduff, informing him that his castle was raided and family killed. In shock Macduff asks if they truly killed his wife and children while he was away, and Malcolm encourages him to seek revenge against Macbeth. Agreeing, Macduff says he must feel his grief and guilt, shouting "sinful Macduff they were struck for thee!" Malcolm further encourages Macduff to use his anger to drive him, to which Macduff agrees, declaring he will not succumb to weeping but rather face "this fiend of Scotland." They depart to begin the attack on Scotland to overthrow Macbeth.

Scene Analysis

Though portrayed as prominent members of the story in previous acts, it is in this scene where Malcolm and Macduff are truly explored as characters with Shakespeare offering insight into their beliefs and what purpose they will serve towards the end of *Macbeth*. Before exploring each, it is interesting to note the placement and length of this scene, as it serves as the longest in the play, clocking in at over two hundred lines. It comes before the highly climactic final act of the play, yet is mainly filled with discussion about Malcolm and Macduff's respective personalities and desires. The purpose of these decisions lie in the concept of the **calm before the storm.** If following Shakespeare's tragic model, Act 4 is meant to be the **respite** after the action of Act 3, and is designed to build tension that will tragically unfold within Act 5. Though not as thematically dense as Macbeth's second meeting with the witches, Malcolm and Macduff's discussion plants the seeds for their eventual rebellion, and for Macduff specifically, underscores his motivation to kill Macbeth.

Respite: a short period of rest or relief.

Continuing with Macduff, though the audience gains a sense of his character from his appearance in Act 2, it is here where we truly understand his emotional state. From his introduction, Macduff is shown to be a devoted loyalist to the Scottish crown, specifically to King Duncan, as his distraught reaction to the violent murder of the king would indicate. Macduff's suspicious nature was also displayed in the same scene, questioning Macbeth's motives for killing the servants before they could even confess if they had killed Duncan. In Act 3, Macduff isn't present at Macbeth's banquet and is rumoured to have fled Scotland in order to seek out Malcolm. In this scene, it becomes clear what Macduff's true views and opinions about Macbeth's rule are, as not only is Macduff loyal to the rightful king of Scotland, but he is also a staunch **patriot**. Numerous times he quotes "bleed, bleed poor country," despairing at what has become of his home. When considering Lady Macduff's plight in the previous scene, Shakespeare makes it clear how deeply devoted Macduff is to Scotland, sacrificing the security of his own family in order to seek someone to restore order to his homeland. Yet Macduff is still presented with the same grey complexity as the other major characters of the text. Macduff's decision to practically abandon his family haunts him, as he knows they were killed to target him, causing him to feel immense grief and heartbreak. Spiritually, Macduff goes as far as to declare himself "sinful Macduff."

Patriot: someone who loves and is deeply loyal to their country.

Melodrama: a sensational dramatic piece with exaggerated characters and emotions.

The **melodrama** Shakespeare is displaying within this scene achieves much in conveying to his audience the consequences of violence. Yet Shakespeare also employs a brutal example of tragic irony with Macduff, as in order for him to fulfil the prophecy of being the only one to kill Macbeth, he must be provoked enough to seek such vengeance. Macduff himself causes such a provocation by fleeing the country and marking his family as traitors.

Tragically, Macduff's loyalty to his country leads to the death of his family but ultimately inspires him to free his country, highlighting the price of destiny and desire to the audience. Though less significant overall than Macduff's role in this scene, the exploration of Malcolm's character is also important in the overall analysis of the play. Except for the brief appearances in earlier acts, Malcolm's character is never granted much attention until now. A seeming afterthought to Macbeth and probably the audience up until this point, Malcolm's behaviour throughout this scene seemingly does little to indicate he will be any great threat to Macbeth. Portrayed as highly emotional and extremely erratic, Malcolm appears to shift moods as the scene progresses, beginning the scene wishing to "weep our sad bosoms empty" and continuing by questioning Macduff's loyalties. At first Malcolm's bizarre behaviour can be perceived as weakness but when considering all that he has gone through, especially the murder of his father, separation from his brother, and exile from his birthright as king, it is easier to sympathise with him.

Furthermore, Malcolm's age may also help explain his self-doubt, as he is likely only a boy. He pretends to admonish himself firstly as lusty, then greedy, and then a whole host of negative things until Macduff loses his temper and shouts at Malcolm about how he is not only not "fit to govern" but not even fit "to live." It is possible that this is an attempt to underscore Malcolm's **propensity** to manipulate, as his self-critical outburst was designed to confirm Macduff's loyalty to him and his family and to seek what Macduff respects in a leader and monarch, specifically **piety** and goodness.

Propensity: a tendency or inclination to act in a certain way.

Piety: the quality of being religious or reverent.

It is curious that the moment Macduff voices such beliefs when mentioning Malcolm's family that his attitude completely changes, renouncing all that he said as a lie and immediately revealing the fact the English are backing him to war. The emotional, self-conscious boy is curiously transformed into a self-assured and confident man, who goes so far as to **goad** Macduff into seeking revenge against Macbeth, mere moments after he showed doubt that he would even want the crown. Maybe it is the shock of the outburst that caused such a change, but considering Shakespeare's clever manipulation and subversion of character throughout the play, Malcolm manipulating Macduff to use as a political tool isn't completely out of the question.

Goad: to provoke or compel someone into action.

Act 5 Scene 1

Scene Summary

The final act begins at Dunsinane Castle with a conversation between a doctor and servant woman. The doctor asks the woman if the rumours of Lady Macbeth's sleepwalking are true. Confirming it so, the doctor is unnerved, quietly stating there is "a great **perturbation** of nature." They are both startled when Lady Macbeth walks into the room, seemingly asleep, holder a light.

Perturbation: a disturbance causing anxiety or mental unease.

Observing her rubbing her hands, the servant says that Lady Macbeth has been observed mimicking the movement of washing her hands. Lady Macbeth begins to speak, distressingly chanting "out damned spot! Out!...who would have thought the old man to have had so much blood in him?" and muttering about dead Lady Macduff. She wonders aloud if her hands will never been clean and if the smell of blood will ever go away. Deeply disturbed, the doctor tells the servant girl this is beyond his knowledge, as Lady Macbeth continues to talk, now reassuring herself, telling herself to "wash your hands, put on your night-gown, look not so pale... Banquo's buried he cannot come out of the grave" before leaving, muttering "what's done cannot be undone." Shaken, the doctor orders the servant to watch carefully over Lady Macbeth, as he hints to knowing of the crimes committed by her and her husband, quietly and ominously quoting, "unnatural deeds do breed unnatural troubles; infected minds." He says goodnight and tells her he dares not speak of what he has just witnessed.

Scene Analysis

The beginning of the final act starts as many of the other act's introductions have, quietly but ominously. This scene centres entirely on plight of Lady Macbeth, who we haven't seen since the dinner with Banquo's ghost. However, her previously confident, manipulative, and scheming demeanour is replaced with with what can only be described as a paranoid and deluded woman wracked with the guilt of her actions. This shift in character serves as the final part of the arc Shakespeare has developed for her, with her initial appearance of the bold, gender-defying politician pulling the strings of Macbeth's ascent being worn away slowly as Macbeth became more and more ambitious, driven by his own desires rather than his wife's. In this scene Shakespeare displays the end result, as ironically as Macbeth is feeling at his most powerful, Lady Macbeth seems to be at her weakest. The notion of guilt is powerful in this scene, and while some may interpret this as a form of punishment Shakespeare doles to a powerful women, this seems more like the natural deterioration of someone dealing with the weight of the horrific actions done to gain such power. Though there may still be elements of sexism present in Shakespeare's writing of Lady Macbeth, when considering the complex nature in which the rest of *Macbeth's* characters are written, it becomes clear there is more to her decline than meets the eye.

Lady Macbeth's delusional behaviour of sleepwalking and talking is highly unnerving, and indicates to the audience that what they're seeing is unnatural. The motif of the natural order of the world being out of balance arises poignantly within this scene, as it is now directly linked to the major theme of guilt that permeates the play, with the doctor himself clarifying this when he quotes, "unnatural deeds do breed unnatural troubles." Initially the guilt Lady Macbeth feels is absent when trying to calm her husband's various outbursts, but like destiny, is absolute and will haunt those who ignore it long enough. Contextually, the highly superstitious and religious crowd would understand the concept of the destructive weight of guilt caused by sinful action. It should not be forgotten that it was Lady Macbeth who created the plan to murder Duncan and physically tampered with the evidence getting the king's blood on her hands. The motif of blood and guilt, associated with Macbeth in that earlier scene, returns in this one as she mimes washes her hands of invisible blood, trying in vain to erase the guilt that poisons her mind.

Though incredibly dormant up until this point, as she lost her power, all that remained was the reality of her actions. In a twisted sense of irony, much like Macbeth's killing of Macduff's family, **the same actions that would secure her power led to her downfall** as the more confident Macbeth became in his position, the more forgotten she was in hers. Though some would say it is well deserved, with Lady Macbeth's partially responsible for the storm of violence and disorder that has plagued Scotland, Shakespeare does not paint her demise as purely just. In fact, Lady Macbeth is almost sympathetic in this scene – a tortured soul desperately trying to repent and rid herself of the guilt that has turned her life into a nightmare, shouting "out spot, out!" at nothing and even trying to repent for the sins her husband's crimes, wondering "the Thane of Fife had a wife. Where is she now?...will these hands never be clean." Though Macbeth's downfall and justice would come soon after, we are left to ponder whether Lady Macbeth truly was a villain, or simply too ambitious, her manipulation of her husband turning on herself as he rose, leaving her a forgotten shadow to carry his grief.

Act 5 Scene 2

Scene Summary

The thanes Menteith, Caithness, Angus, and Lennox all meet upon a field with their soldiers. Menteith tells them the English army is near, lead by Malcolm, Siward, and Macduff, and that revenge burns deeply within them all. Angus confirms they are near Birnam Wood, as Caithness questions if Donalbain is with them. Lennox tells him no, but Siward has brought his young son with him so that he can experience battle and become a man. Menteith asks what is happening with Macbeth, referring to him as "tyrant." Caithness informs them that he is fortifying Dunsinane castle, spreading the rumour that Macbeth has gone mad. Angus approves of the rumour, declaring "now how does he feel, his secret murders sticking on his hands." Satisfied, the thanes declare to march, as they move to join their army to Malcolm's at Birnam Wood.

Scene Analysis

The second scene of this act introduces the pattern that can observed when analysing the final moments of the play. Act 5 is the second and final climax of the text, so it must weave together the various storylines of the play for the text to have a satisfactory, albeit tragic ending. *Macbeth*'s final act alternates between Macbeth's and his enemies' perspectives. In the case of this scene, the audience views the rebellious thanes' actions as they plan to join forces with Malcolm. Not much thematically can be gained here, but the scene serves nicely to highlight the consequences of Macbeth's actions and foreshadow important things to come. Once again Macbeth is referred to simply as "tyrant," truly showing how far he has fallen in the eyes of his once loyal thanes. Contextually, Macbeth being called a tyrant, no matter how accurate, would have been a sign of immense disrespect and indicates his rule has been so poor and cruel for the term tyrant was not one used without warrant in the play's context. The text still does not reveal exactly what Macbeth has done, with the thanes only hinting at Macbeth's cruel actions, so there still is a question of how truly troubled his rule was, with only the annihilation of Macduff's family and Banquo as evidence.

Aside from the political aspect, there is some subtle foreshadowing occurring in this scene with the thanes discussing Birnam Wood as the site of the rebel army meeting. The mere mention of Birnam Wood, so closely associated with prophecy and specifically Macbeth's downfall, would be a hint to the audience of the climax to come, heightening the dramatic tension.

Act 5 Scene 3
Scene Summary
Back at Dunsinane castle, Macbeth orders that no more news be reported to him. He dismisses Malcolm as a boy born of a woman and says he will not feel fear until Birnam Wood reaches his walls, echoing the witches' prophecy. A servant enters telling him that Malcolm's army consists of ten thousand soldiers, but Macbeth angrily dismisses him. He calls for his servant Seyton as he wonders about the battle to come. He thinks that this battle will either secure his reign for a long time to come or end it, reflecting that he has lived long enough and that the honour and love reserved for those in his age and position are lost to him forever, with only curses and fear replacing them. He feels his heart wishes to end it all and commit suicide but he cannot bring himself to do it. Seyton then arrives, and Macbeth asks him to bring him his armour, also ordering Seyton to send more cavalry out to hang those who are afraid. Turning to the doctor, Macbeth asks how his wife is, to which the doctor responds it is not a physical ailment that troubles her but the visions she suffers that keep her from sleep. Not impressed, Macbeth demands he cure her of the visions, stating "canst thou not minister to a mind diseased," essentially asking him to use drugs to cure her. The doctor tells him it is up to the patient to cure her mind and Macbeth laughs asking if the doctor can heal his country. He nervously tells Macbeth that his military preparations are a cure, but the king ignores him as he calls for Seyton to follow him with the armour, boldly stating "I will not be afraid of death and bane, till Birnam Forest come to Dunsinane" before leaving. Alone, the doctor wishes he were anywhere else than Dunsinane and claims he would never come back no matter how much they paid him.

Scene Analysis
These scene approaches the lowest point of Macbeth's character arc. Practically displaying no remorse or even emotion in this scene, Macbeth is portrayed as a raving madman, so confident in the ridiculous nature of the witches' second set of prophecies that he declares himself unafraid of death and basically invincible. The once quiet and thoughtful thane, who felt overwhelmed at the sudden promise of power he had achieved and suffered from near crippling guilt at the thought of killing a single man, has been warped by Shakespeare into a cruel despot, ordering the killing of those who spread fear of the coming battle and ignoring his wife's mental anguish. Though he shows a brief sense of wanting an end, his pride and thoughts of destiny keep him from further acting on such beliefs. It speaks volumes to Shakespeare's ability as a writer that Macbeth, a man morally so far gone he is hated by his entire country and believes himself invincible, can still show some sympathetic self-doubt. If the argument that Macbeth is a tragic hero is to be believed, then this scene with Macbeth displaying an immense amount of hubris is crucial, as his downfall from his fatal flaws comes swiftly after this scene.

Act 5 Scene 4

Scene Summary

At Birnam Wood, the rebellious Scottish thanes meet with Malcolm's joint Scottish and English army. Malcolm greets them and tells the thanes that the time will soon come when their homes will be safe once more. Malcolm orders that every solider is to cut a branch off the trees and place it upon them, so that their true numbers are hidden when marching upon Macbeth. Siward tells them that Macbeth remains at Dunsinane Castle and is waiting for the approaching army. Malcolm is pleased to know this, as more and more of his allies are fleeing from him in revolt with the only ones staying being those who holds captive. Satisfied with what they have done and heard at Birnam Wood, they continue to march upon Dunsinane.

Scene Analysis

Another brief scene away from Dunsinane, much like scenes later that focus on Malcolm's march to Macbeth, there isn't much to dissect within this moment of the play, though that's not to say this scene is not important, as it is here at Birnam Wood that Shakespeare reveals to his audience the clever and tragic way that the prophecy will be fulfilled (as well as subtly invoking the theme of deceptive appearances). Ever since Macbeth heard the prophecies, Shakespeare has made it abundantly clear that these visions of the future should not be taken at face value. Macbeth does not heed these warnings, of course, letting his ambition obscure his caution, and it is these blind desires and lack of foresight that the witches prey upon, and that Malcolm benefits from when conspiring to bring Macbeth down.

Act 5 Scene 5

Scene Summary

The play returns to Dunsinane as Macbeth orders his servants banners to be placed on the outside walls to stop cowardice. He is satisfied in his defences, willing to wait out a siege while his enemies starve, and says if so many had not deserted him, he could have face them in open combat. A woman's cry rings out and Macbeth orders Seyton to investigate it. To himself, Macbeth thinks it has been along time since he was afraid, that there was once a time where a woman's shriek would have unnerved him but after all he has done and witnessed, he is too familiar with horror to be afraid. Seyton returns with the news that Lady Macbeth has died. Strangely calm, Macbeth reflects she would have died in time if it hadn't happened today and begins his soliloquy. "Tomorrow and tomorrow and tomorrow" he quietly starts, continuing by discussing the futility of time and life. He envisions life like the shadow of a candle, a "a walking shadow, a poor player that struts and frets his hour upon the stage... it is a tale told by an idiot, full of sound and fury signifying nothing." After this, a messenger approaches telling him Birnam Wood walks upon the castle. Shocked and enraged, he calls the messenger a liar, but the man insists he looks upon his walls to see. Steadying himself, Macbeth shouts for his soldiers to go forward to fight as there is no point in running or staying, for he has grown tired of life and wishes for chaos and death in battle.

Scene Analysis

At first glance this scene blends in with the others of Act 5, switching to Macbeth overseeing Dunsinane's defences in his defiance of Malcolm. This also contains one of Shakespeare's most profound soliloquies. Macbeth's "Tomorrow and tomorrow and tomorrow" speech is one of the most influential in literary history and offers deep insight not only into Macbeth's character but the human condition in general. Its inclusion in the play serves to further the tragic narrative being told, as it is one of the only quiet and thoughtful moments granted to its characters, focusing not on political war or supernatural destiny, but rather the humanity of these characters. This whole scene analysis will be dedicated to breaking it down and understanding its importance to the play.

The scene begins with Macbeth as confident as ever, feeling invincible against the coming threat of Malcolm. It is only when he hears the shriek of a woman that the confident persona begins to falter as he thinks about the nature of fear and how he has "almost forgot the taste of fears." Shakespeare successfully creates a sense of unease and dread here, as this single scream of a woman must be significant to unnerve Macbeth, a man who is quoted as saying "I have supped full with horrors." When recalling Lady Macbeth's strange condition in Act 5, Scene 1, the audience is able to come to dark conclusions about her fate. Once again, Shakespeare's ability to write compelling horror is evident, as the use of the unknown makes the audience uneasy as to what is to come and Macbeth's reaction all the more compelling. When finding out it was his wife, unlike the mad raving and paranoia after Duncan's death or the cool indifference to Young Siward's later on in the act, Macbeth seems merely shocked and empty at the news. His first line of "she should have died hereafter" almost seems like he was expecting Lady Macbeth to die and whether it was that very day or sometime after, it did not matter. Taken at face value it appears that Macbeth is cold to his wife's death with this line and does not care, yet Shakespeare's exploration of his hopelessness makes this a somewhat relatable reaction to the death of a loved one. Macbeth seemingly tries to accept his wife's apparent suicide as inevitable in order to move on as quickly as possible from his pain, grief, and guilt, yet realistically he falters and the pretence of invincibility he has built since receiving his second batch prophecies shatters.

With his psychological defences destroyed, Macbeth begins his soliloquy with an ambiguous line, "she should have died hereafter." This could be seen as his baseless belief that she was not meant to die that day, suggesting that even though he had received no such prophecy, Macbeth was fully invested in his own conception of destiny. However, we can also interpret this as a callous remark about how she would have died eventually, so what would it matter whether it was "tomorrow" or the day after?

The whole play up until this point has consisted of Macbeth and Lady Macbeth doing everything in their power, without caring about consequence, to ensure Macbeth's destiny to be king. Their path was one of violence, murder, betrayal, and sorcery, breaking oaths against humanity and the natural world. While it seems Macbeth's character gained strength by ignoring the repercussions of his actions, Lady Macbeth was seemingly so consumed by her guilt from the pursuit of power that it drove her to guilt-ridden madness and eventually implied suicide.

It is the death of the one who rose equally as brutally beside him and the woman he loved that breaks Macbeth, as due to Banquo's prophecy, he knows he will not have children to follow him, his last justification for his actions outside of his ambition is gone. Shakespeare uses her death as lesson for his audience on the effects guilt from evil deeds can do, but in the context of Macbeth, Lady Macbeth's death is a reminder of the fragility of life and how important purpose can be. He declares, "out, out, brief candle," as he realises that his last true ally and confidant is gone.

The next section of the soliloquy goes on to highlight this point further while also showcasing Shakespeare's masterful use of imagery to weave its message. Macbeth goes on to describe life in many ways, "a walking shadow... a poor player that struts and frets on the stage and then is heard no more," each holding some symbolic meaning. The imagery of the shadow, first and foremost, infers themes of action and consequence, with Macbeth himself casting a long and dark shadow on the pages of Shakespeare's history. Shakespeare possibly uses the shadow as another reference to the fragility of life, as a shadow is only a visual reflection of a person and disappears almost as quickly as it appears. In reference to the player, it appears Shakespeare is breaking the forth wall and Macbeth himself realises for a brief moment he is character in a tragedy, doomed from the beginning to meet a tragic end. The most powerful of these images however is Macbeth's final line in the soliloquy: "it is a tale told by an idiot, full of sound and fury, signifying nothing."

There is so much meaning and power in that single line that an entire essay can be dedicated to answering the questions it raises. Who is the idiot Macbeth is referring to? Himself? The audience? Shakespeare? Why is this person an idiot? Is it something they did? Is there something they don't know? Is the tale life? Why is it described as so messy and angry? Why does such emotion signify nothing? If it is a tale being told then is it truly signifying nothing? These are the questions lying at the heart of this soliloquy and truly display the futility Macbeth feels at this point in the play at his situation. Shakespeare, through these twelve lines, manages to create something so immensely profound that it speaks volumes to the themes of his play. The importance of this soliloquy cannot be understated as its near infinite amounts of interpretation can be applied to *Macbeth*'s themes.

Act 5 Scene 6

Scene Summary

Malcolm's army arrives at Dunsinane Castle. Malcolm orders his soldiers to throw down their disguises made from the branches of Birnam Wood to show Macbeth their true numbers. He orders Siward and his son to lead the first attack, while he and Macduff are to continue the rest of their plan. Siward wishes them luck, as Macduff orders trumpets to be sounded to warn of the blood and death to come.

Scene Analysis

This is one of the shortest scenes in the play, and other than showing the audience Malcolm's arrival to Dunsinane and the final stand of Macbeth, this scene offers very little thematically or symbolically. Rather it is the release of the tension brewed throughout the rest of the play and serves as the exciting action portion of Shakespeare's tragic formula.

Act 5 Scene 7

Scene Summary

Within Dunsinane Macbeth finds himself surrounded by enemies but refuses to flee, thinking himself invincible still believing the prophecy that no man born of a woman can kill him. Young Siward, Siward's son, enters, and after boldly challenging Macbeth, Young Siward fights him only to be killed quickly. Scoffing at the young man's foolish attempt to slay him, he leaves taking Young Siward's body with him. Macduff soon arrives shouting for Macbeth to reveal himself, claiming if he does not kill Macbeth his "wife and children's ghosts will haunt me still." Malcolm and Siward join, with Siward telling him the castle is nearly fallen and the thanes have shown great bravery in the fighting, with the day nearly won. With that they all enter further into the castle.

Scene Analysis

Much like the previous scene, this one is short and simple, though the death of Young Siward is worth analysing. Macbeth has repeatedly been responsible for destroying family bonds – by killing Duncan and Banquo, he leaves Malcolm/Donalbain and Fleance fatherless, and by killing Macduff's son and Young Siward, he robs two men of their sons. Not only does this underscore Macbeth's brutality and subversion of the natural order, but it also draws attention to who is left in the wake of these deaths, mourning their loved ones. Meanwhile, Macbeth has no son, and with Lady Macbeth gone, we can infer that no one will mourn the loss of the tyrannical king, which makes Macduff's execution of Macbeth more justifiable in restoring order to the kingdom.

Act 5 Scene 8

Scene Summary

Briefly alone, Macbeth states he will not kill himself like the ancient Roman warriors did, but will instead keep fighting. Macduff enters, finally confronting the man who killed his family. Macbeth admits he had been avoiding Macduff since slaughtering his wife and child. The battle commences. During their fight, Macbeth tells Macduff it is futile to fight him as he cannot be killed by one born of a woman. Cursing Macbeth, Macduff reveals he was ripped from his mother's womb when he was born. Macbeth's courage is destroyed as he tells Macduff the spirits lied to him with their carefully worded prophecies and he wishes to not fight Macduff anymore. Macduff demands he yield and if he does, they will make a mockery of him, hanging a painted sign saying "here may you see the tyrant" around his neck.

Hearing that, Macbeth refuses to surrender as he will not "kiss the ground before young Malcolm's feet" and though Birnam Wood has come to Dunsinane and he is fighting a man unborn of a woman, he will fight until the end, calling to Macduff to continue and damning the man who cries out in surrender first. They clash once again as the scene ends.

(Though in some editions this scene is combined with Scene 9, for the purposes of this analysis, Scene 8 ends here and is the penultimate scene of *Macbeth*.)

Scene Analysis

The last time Macbeth is seen alive, this scene serves to truly portray how far Macbeth's character has fallen. The Macbeth of the first act was not the man duelling with Macduff in this scene. Shakespeare introduced a brave, somewhat ambitious but cautious man, who doubted and felt guilt at the temptation of power. Yet throughout the play, Macbeth's guilt was overridden by his ambition, which caused him to be manipulated by his scheming wife, seek dark forces to ensure his destiny, and murder those innocent of any wrongdoing other than being a threat to his unjust power. Yet as he stands on the brink of defeat, having lost his wife, his allies, and based on his soliloquy, even his will to live, he remains defiant.

Though the "tomorrow" soliloquy presents Macbeth as a man who has given up on life, Shakespeare seems to contradict that sentiment at the beginning of this scene in which Macbeth rhetorically asks "why should I play the Roman fool and die on mine own sword?" It appears that Macbeth is aware he could kill himself and give himself a tragic end like many ancient heroes, but rather than grant Macbeth an end befitting of a tragic hero, Shakespeare has Macbeth fight on, causing more bloodshed, driven by defiance and arrogance at his own invincibility. Macbeth's inner goodness and humanity, no matter how corrupted, died with his wife. The man facing Macduff and refusing to bow to Malcolm is a mere shell of the man who once was.

While this scene offers insight into Macbeth's character, it also serves to explore Macduff. The news of the death of his family appears to have shifted his motivations to fight Macbeth from freeing Scotland to pure vengeance. Macduff killing Macbeth not only fulfils the witches' prophecy with a clever twist befitting Shakespeare's style, but completes his arc as Macbeth's foil while simultaneously acting as a physical representation of the theme of violence. Both men are stubborn and driven by violence, and without his inner humanity, Macduff would simply be fighting the pure mirror of himself. Yet whereas Macbeth only fights for his own pride, Macduff fights for his dead family and all those who Macbeth wronged and killed.

Macduff therefore breaks the cycle of violence that Macbeth began, as not only does Macbeth die without an heir, but Macduff silences Macbeth's reign by fighting for the righteous cause, and thus is justified in killing the king, in an ironic parallel to Macbeth killing Duncan solely for the kingship and not for any grander purpose about the good of the realm. This is a testament to Macduff's strength of character – instead of simply taking the crown for himself and continuing cycle of bloodshed after killing Macbeth, he grants it to the younger and more inexperienced Malcolm, trusting in him to be a good leader. Such poetic justice is fitting for the end of a Shakespearean tragedy as Macduff seemingly puts an end to the prophecies, violence, and political instability.

Act 5 Scene 9

Scene Summary

Malcolm, Siward, and the thanes all enter and discuss their victory. Malcolm wishes some of his men could have survived the battle but Siward assures him it is the nature of war and their casualties low anyway. Malcolm questions to where Macduff and Young Siward are, with Ross giving the bad news, telling Siward that his son is dead but he died like a true solider. Asking if he died of wounds taken on his front, when confirmed Siward claims if he had "as many sons as I have hairs" then he would not wish for a more honourable death for any of them. Macduff enters carrying Macbeth's bloody head and hailing Malcolm as king of Scotland. The rest of his thanes cheer the same, as Malcolm begins his speech, declaring a new age for Scotland. He rewards his thanes by declaring them as the first earls of Scotland and calling for their exiled allies to return home to a freed land. He shouts to bring justice to all those who aided the tyrant Macbeth and his cruel queen, who is rumoured to have taken her own life, and to rebuild with the blessing of God in the right times and places to come. He thanks them once more and invites his new earls to his coronation, ending the play.

Scene Analysis

Catharsis: releasing and providing relief from strong or repressed emotions.

At the end of the text, the play is expected to resolve the overarching conflicts and provide an ending suitable for its characters and plot. Unless there is a direct sequel, this is how most texts should end. Being a Shakespearean tragedy, there should also be a sense of **catharsis** and thematic release. To elaborate, the concept of tragic catharsis is that of an **emotional purification at the end of the tragedy** – a final realisation typically reserved for a tragic hero. In the case of *Macbeth* however, the lines of who is a true tragic hero are blurred, as throughout this analysis the debate as to whether Macbeth is a tragic hero or simply just a villain is prominent to his interpretation as a character and the play's thematic choices. Regardless, without a clear tragic hero to take the role of the catharsis, Shakespeare instead uses Malcolm, a character portrayed as just and righteous in his cause, to present the final cathartic declaration. Yet unlike other tragic finales, instead of a philosophical speech centring around learning from the hero's fatal flaw, Malcolm's speech is decidedly more political in its nature, in which he denounces the previous rule, referring to Macbeth as a tyrant, and promising to bring justice rather than warning against any particular themes such as violence and ambition.

The reasoning behind this choice may be attributed to Shakespeare treating *Macbeth* differently than his other tragedies. From the very beginning he made clear to create a much different atmosphere than his typical high society settings of tragedies such as *Othello* and *Romeo and Juliet,* instead creating a dark and dreary setting, accurate in its brutality and grimness to its 11th century context.

Rather than create morally black-and-white characters, set either as good or evil, he experiments and allows his characters to shift and grow, with Macbeth and Lady Macbeth almost reversing personalities as the play progresses. Instead of displaying conflict through the eyes of a few noblemen, *Macbeth* shows the consequences of claiming power and the true nature of war spawned from it, with many young men losing their lives represented by the death of Young Siward. While taking obvious liberties compared to the historical context, Shakespeare ultimately intended for his play to end much like the real history with Malcolm ascending the throne. Politically this was favourable, as Scottish-born King James I, Shakespeare's royal patron, claimed descendance from Banquo's son Fleance, and so would have preferred an ending where the true king reclaimed the throne and the pretender was cast aside and killed for his misdeeds.

The final scene, and Malcolm's speech in particular, also show evidence of increasing English prominence within the Scottish setting, as his declaration of "my thanes and kinsmen henceforth be earls, the first that ever that Scotland in such honour be named" is clear evidence of Malcolm and by extension Shakespeare, trying to 'anglicise' his Scottish subjects. The political intention behind the decision is clear when considering the context, as Shakespeare himself was an Englishman and sought to promote English power and values, seen as nobler than other foreign beliefs, through his play. On an even higher political level, the linking of English and Scottish forces would have pleased King James, as it was a fictional and metaphorical example of what was occurring in 17th century England, as King James settled in as king of both Scotland and England.

Finally, before wrapping up the analysis, it is important to highlight the overall messages Shakespeare was trying to promote to his audience through this incredible text. Macbeth at its heart is a story of **humanity in conflict with itself**. As author William Faulkner once said, "the only thing worth writing about is the human heart in conflict with itself" – a sentiment echoed through *Macbeth*'s very essence. Macbeth's personal story of unbridled ambition leading to a dark path of violence, paranoia, and eventually death is the story of the heart in conflict with itself. Lady Macbeth's desire to seize power and rid herself of her gender expectation only to be stricken by guilt-ridden madness at the reality of her desires is the story of the heart in conflict with itself. Macduff's struggle between his loyalty to his country or family and the destructive consequences of choosing is a struggle of the heart in conflict with itself. Though presenting warnings against seeking answers beyond the natural world and existential ideas of destiny and power, *Macbeth* at its core, is **a story of human tragedy, "full of sound and fury," born by its wild and uncontrollable nature.**

Section 4

Character Analysis

Macbeth

One of Shakespeare's great protagonists, the character of Macbeth is one steeped in complexity and tragedy. A warrior, a thane, a king, and then a tyrant, Macbeth's character is amongst literature's finest and is a shining example of Shakespeare's ability to craft a tragic figure. Based on a real king of Scotland and the wars he fought to claim the throne, Shakespeare's Macbeth is no mere king, as this character goes beyond anything expected of such a role, delving into the unknown and dark world of the supernatural to represent grand themes of power, destiny, and ambition. Whether you consider him a monster or hero, there is much to discuss about the eponymous character of the play.

The major question that should be answered in regards to Macbeth is whether he is **a tragic hero or simply a villain.** Firstly, let's define what a tragic hero is – according to Aristotle, this is a character who carries a fatal flaw that leads to their tragic but deserved death when they realise their wrongdoing. Certainly Macbeth's unrelenting ambition serves as his fatal flaw, as he gradually becomes blinded by the power he receives. It is only when everyone abandons him, even his wife driven to madness and implied suicide, that he finally repents before meeting his end in battle. Macbeth's soliloquy is the strongest piece of evidence supporting Macbeth as a tragic hero, as Macbeth's rumination on the nature of life and its futility are fitting of the often-introspective nature of a tragic hero realising the errors of his ways. His line "it is a tale told by an idiot, full of sound and fury signifying nothing" can be interpreted as Macbeth finally realising the **pointlessness of his pursuit for power** and coming to terms with the crimes he has committed. Macbeth the tragic hero is a character for the audience to realise their own folly and encourage to give up their own petty ambitions. He is a man **twisted and blinded by evil forces of darkness that exist within him to commit horrific acts** and eventually receives an end befitting his crimes.

Now with that perspective established, it is now time to analyse Macbeth as a villain. Though pushed into a prophecy claiming he will be king and having doubts about murdering his king and kinsman Duncan, Macbeth still *decides* to do it, for it seems he has control over his actions and decisions. He chooses to stay and listen to the witches. He chooses to listen to his wife and to kill the king. He chooses to kill the servants so they do not reveal his murder. He chooses to blame the death of the king on Malcolm and Donalbain. He chooses to kill Banquo and attempt to kill his son Fleance to maintain power. He chooses, even after seeing the ghost of the friend he had murdered, to not only visit the witches again, but believe himself invincible from their prophecy then using the confidence gained from it to kill his enemy's entire family as punishment for treason. And finally, when all have abandoned him, his prophecies have betrayed him, and his wife kills herself, he still refuses to surrender nobly and meet a just punishment. This is the path Macbeth chose to follow.

Macbeth throughout the whole play is depicted as a suspicious and paranoid man, not out of guilt but rather fear of punishment. Quotes such as "Prince of Cumberland, that is a step on which I must fall down or else overleap" and "if it were done when its done, then 'twere done quickly" highlight the scheming nature of Macbeth even before the murder and his cruel declarations of "hang those who talk of fear" and "seize upon Fife and give the edge of the sword to his wife and babes" display the monster Macbeth has become.

Though both valid, there are flaws in each of these interpretations, the major one being that both are too absolutist and simplistic. Shakespeare does not create a simple world in *Macbeth* – rather, it is one filled ambivalence, as many of his characters are simply not good nor evil but rather results of their natural human emotions and desires, and that is how Macbeth should be perceived. There are obvious Aristotelean influences with his character, and there is enough evidence to mark him as somewhat heroic, but that does not take away from the fact that Macbeth has unsavoury aspects to his personality, namely his ambition and the arrogance and cruelty that derives from it.

Whether pondering if the ocean can ever wash away his crime of killing Duncan or having his guilt possibly manifest itself as Banquo's ghost in front of him, it is clear Macbeth is suffering from the psychological ramifications of his actions. Much like the tragic hero argument, Macbeth's "tomorrow" soliloquy can help justify this middle path, as its words can be interpreted simply as those of a man who has lost everything but the pride to remain defiant. It can be argued that Macbeth did die a tragic hero's death, and that the real human Macbeth died with his soliloquy, finally coming to peace with his life and actions, and **the man who was killed by Macduff was a hollow shell,** the "the sound and fury" he described.

Lady Macbeth

A devious manipulator. A woman ahead of her time. A tragic figure plagued by guilt. An associate to **regicide,** murder, and tyranny. These are all the ways Lady Macbeth can be described from reading the play. Possibly the most complex and interesting of all of Shakespeare's characters in general, Lady Macbeth is a pinnacle of character work, as she is still studied and debated today as either one of literature's great villains or most tragic figures. Lady Macbeth's impact on the play is immense as she not only influences the politics of Scotland during the duration of the play but also defies her gender role and represents an array of themes and ideas, including gender, guilt, ambition, and power. For starters, as she is a woman in a male-dominated political landscape, created by Shakespeare who lived in a society in which women held very little political power, it is surprising just how influential Lady Macbeth is.

Regicide: killing a king.

Trusted enough to receive politically important letters from her husband, such as the one detailing the prophecy, Lady Macbeth is obviously highly intelligent and even before the events of the play served as a trusted figure to her husband. Furthermore, she formulates the entire plan to kill Duncan and for Macbeth to usurp the throne.

Aside from this cunning nature, Shakespeare in the early stages of her character provides a very powerful desire to be beyond what she perceives herself to be. In an incredibly progressive and powerful way, Shakespeare has her desiring to renounce her gender, having her darkly proclaim, "come, you spirits that tend on mortal thoughts, unsex me here." An incredibly iconic line, it says much about her relationship with her femininity, as when compared to the motherly and devoted Lady Macduff, Lady Macbeth is a driven woman obsessed with raising her and her husband's position.

This desire to go beyond her gender expectations is expanded on further as the play progresses, as she frequently admonishes her husband for his lack of ambition and mocks him of his fears after murdering Duncan and claiming to have seen Banquo's ghost. She goes so far as to physically be involved with the murder, as she returns to the crime scene bearing the bloody daggers that killed Duncan and wipes them on the clothes of the drugged servants in order to blame them. The noble lady wife of the second most powerful man in Scotland returns to her terrified husband with hands covered in blood. This is a powerful move for any character, let alone a female character, and justifies her enduring relevance over four hundred years after the play was written.

At heart, regardless of her actions, Lady Macbeth is a tragic figure. Desiring power beyond what she can obtain, she is forced to resort to dark methods and manipulation in order to achieve even just a taste of what she desires. Yet, this is a cursed achievement, and she is doomed by destiny and forces beyond her understanding. How could such a strong willed and seemingly powerful character turn out such a way? The answer lies in the themes of power and guilt, and the parallel rise of her husband compared to her decline. Initially, Lady Macbeth held immense sway over her husband pushing him against his initial will and morality to fulfil his destiny and even went so far to berate him at times. Yet ironically, as Macbeth became more and more arrogant in his own power, hers declined as she was less informed of her husband's plans, kept in the dark about the murder of Banquo, the second visit to the witches, and the murder of Macduff's family. Whatever phantom power she felt she had was taken from her, leaving her lone with the guilt of the actions that eventually lead her and husband into a position of being despised and betrayed by their enemies. This is why she is a tragic and brilliant figure of literature, as though she was partially responsible of her own ambition, she had no knowledge of how the same ambition would twist her husband and eventually ruin her life. **In a haunting case of tragic irony, the very thing Lady Macbeth desired led to her demise.**

Duncan

Though brief, King Duncan's time in the play serves to not only put into motion the tragedy to come but also to highlight the dark nature of the themes of violence and guilt once his death comes. Far from the most complex of characters, the audience gets the picture that Duncan is **a good man and a magnanimous king, but not a strong one.** From his often praising and kind words, it is clear his loyal subjects follow him due to being a good person rather than fearing him as their absolute ruler. This aspect provides an interesting contrast compared to his successor Macbeth, as due to the guilt and paranoia of murdering Duncan, he could never be the type of king Duncan was, resorting to rule through tyranny as his own power wasn't as secure as Duncan's. This is a pattern that emerges over and over again with Duncan throughout the play, as in typical Shakespearean irony, it is only after his death that Duncan's influence as king is truly felt.

Magnanimous: generous or forgiving.

Subsequently, Duncan's death is a major component of the downward spiral of Macbeth's reign and sanity. The most obvious example of this is the suspicion, exile, and eventual rebellion by Duncan's son and named heir Malcolm who leads the army with Macduff and Siward that eventually overthrows and kills Macbeth. That is only on the explicit level however, as Duncan's death had much deeper, much more thematic impacts on the characters throughout the play. One example is the guilt felt by Macbeth and eventually Lady Macbeth in the lead up and direct aftermath of his murder, with Macbeth wondering about the spiritual and political consequences of killing not only his king but his kinsman, stating "we still have judgement here that we but teach bloody instructions which being taught return to plague the inventor" before eventually succumbing to his ambition and killing him. For Lady Macbeth, Shakespeare uses the motif of Duncan's physical blood being a mark of her guilt, as in her mad sleeping walking state she ominously alludes the murder stating "who would have thought the old man to have had so much blood in him?" before allegedly committing suicide. Yet, though Duncan leaves in his wake fear and darkness in the form of Macbeth, he also inspires courage and loyalty even beyond his death. The memory of the good king leads the thanes to side with Malcolm to end Macbeth's tyranny and it is Macduff's scathing quote to Malcolm stating he is "fit to govern, no... thy royal father was a most sainted king" reminding him of the man his was to break him from his crippling self-doubt. Shakespeare goes as far to imply that nature itself was right when Duncan lived, as after his death the thane Ross notes mysterious and dark things occurring in the world. Duncan was the **epitome** of goodness within the play, and basically the sacrificial lamb for the tragedy to enfold – **a good king, Shakespeare implies, holds order within the world.**

Epitome: the perfect example or embodiment of something.

Macduff

Macduff, Thane of Fife, is amongst the most complex characters of the play as his various personal motivations and beliefs come in conflict with the morality of the world and thus make him **conduit** for the tragedy Shakespeare depicts. Introduced as loyal, just, and honest, from his first appearance in Act 2, Macduff immediately serves to contrast to Macbeth, and subtly hints as his role as Macbeth's foil and eventual downfall. Yet these contrasting traits are the same that lead him to abandon his family and condemn them to Macbeth's wrath, specifically his loyalty to his homeland and King Duncan. In some sense, Macduff is the true tragic hero of the play, not Macbeth.

Conduit: a channel through which the author conveys something.

When justifying this argument, it is important to go back and analyse Macduff's role as a foil to Macbeth and how it relates to the tragedy. The definition of a foil is almost a mirror to the protagonist except for a few crucial aspects. At the beginning of the play, Macbeth and Macduff find themselves in nearly the exact same position as thanes under the rule of King Duncan. It is only when Macbeth wins renown in battle that he begins to rise over Macduff, a fact not respected by Macduff as the play progresses. Position isn't the only thing that separates the two men though, as Macduff's loyalty and respect for the crown of Scotland contrasts greatly with Macbeth's murderous destruction of the kingdom. This is particularly evident when the two thanes see Duncan's body: Macduff breaks down in feelings of grief he cannot even articulate, whilst Macbeth is preoccupied with shifting the blame by framing the servants he also murdered. Contrasting Macbeth's deception to Macduff's honesty is a powerful means for Shakespeare to establish this foil relationship, and implicitly ties to the motif of the known and unknown.

Macduff's loyalty to Duncan sows seeds of doubt in his mind, and hence he does not attend Macbeth's coronation, fleeing to seek the exiled Prince Malcolm. Although the audience sees this as justifiable and even perceptive, this is ultimately what leads to tragic deaths of his family who are at the mercy of the tyrant Macbeth. Lady Macduff declares her husband's "flight was madness" and she even tells their son "your father is dead" while Macduff is desperately trying to restore the kingdom by persuading Malcolm to declare war. His mental anguish is **exacerbated** when his family is slaughtered by Macbeth, as punishment for Macduff's treason against him. This makes Macduff profoundly sympathetic as not only was he faced with the divided loyalties to his kingdom and his family, he chose to act in the country's best interests even if it meant putting his family in danger. However, Macduff's character is not tragic just because he loses his family because of his loyalty. He is tragic because when considering the overarching ideas of destiny and Macduff's role in Macbeth's second set of prophecies, **these horrific events that happen to him are part of some grand uncontrollable scheme by powers beyond his comprehension.**

Exacerbated: to make a bad situation even worse.

Macduff is a pawn of fate, born through the tragic and violent loss from his mother to be destined to kill Macbeth, but only given the energy and the ability to do so when he must make himself a traitor that leads to his own family's demise. If there were ever a character in Shakespeare's texts that perfectly embodies tragedy, it is Macduff. He is a perfect foil, and it is no wonder that Macduff was the one Shakespeare chose to slay Macbeth.

Banquo

Banquo, thane to King Duncan of Scotland and companion to Macbeth, is among the play's most important characters. Noble, honest, and wary, Banquo is one of the play's purely good characters and his death is a turning point the play in both plot and theme. Much like Duncan, it is only after his death that Banquo's impact is felt throughout the play, as the ghost of his memory and his physical manifestation haunt Macbeth.

Banquo's curiosity is displayed almost immediately when he demands to receive his own visions from the witches. However, upon receiving the knowledge that he will "be lesser than Macbeth and greater" and his line will breed kings, Banquo is far more sceptical and measured than Macbeth as Shakespeare suggests he is less inclined to seek glory at all costs. Eventually, he is killed for the threat he poses to Macbeth, and although Banquo is smart enough to fear that Macbeth "played most foully for" the title of king, he is not quick enough to escape Macbeth's hired assassins.

Subsequently, **the ghost of Banquo, whether real or not, represents the true importance of his character, as it is a symbol of the evil of Macbeth's deed and its consequence for those who seek power at all costs.** Never speaking, never gesturing, Banquo's ghost is a lingering reminder for Macbeth and the audience that there are always consequences for one's actions, even beyond the physical realm. If Banquo's ghost is believed to be a simple figment of Macbeth's imagination, then it represents the oppressive nature of guilt in the play.

If a genuine spirit, then the ghost is Shakespeare's reflection of the dark nature of the supernatural, with its gruesome **visage** and ominous presence. Lending to the belief that the spirit is real is the fact Macbeth sees it once more in the cave after his second set of prophecies, and represents Hecate's ultimate punishment for Macbeth daring to defy destiny, as the ghost is a constant reminder of Banquo's prophecy. Even though Banquo is dead, he still fulfils the prophecy by securing the escape of his son Fleance, alive and safe out of Macbeth's reach. Literarily this is a good example of Shakespeare's use of symbolism and foreshadowing, but Banquo also has a political function as King James of England, Shakespeare's patron, claimed descendance from Banquo's line, so his inclusion within the play was one of not only literary importance but socio-political importance as well.

Visage: a person's face or appearance.

The Witches

The strangest of *Macbeth*'s major characters, the Weird Sisters are the heart of the play's supernatural nature and the catalyst for the tragedy to come. Described as bent over and ugly, the witches punish the innocent for small slights, yet Shakespeare portrays them as powerful, malicious figures, not to be underestimated or disrespected. It can be argued that the witches are the true villains of the text, as it is their prophecies to Macbeth that lead to the bloodshed and tragedy.

Yet to simply dismiss the witches as mere villains is to fail to grasp their true role within the text. Shakespeare uses the witches as **agents of the unknown and representatives to his audience about the incomprehensible nature of the supernatural and destiny.** Not complex from a pure character standpoint, the important aspects of their characters lie in their actions and the purpose they serve for the audience. The latter statement is easier to explain, as Shakespeare clearly intended to create an uneasy and dread-filled atmosphere for his audience to highlight that all the injustice and bloodshed in the play is from natural, and the use of the witches would have frankly terrified his 17th century audience.

The theme of destiny is crucial to the interpretation of the play and by extension the characters of the witches. The witches receive such power of prophecy from their master the goddess Hecate, who admonishes them for their casual use of it on men such as Macbeth. This raises a significant question regarding their true motives and intentions: are they giving such destructive prophecies out of maliciousness, or are they agents of destiny? Many lean towards the first interpretation, as not only does Hecate admonish them but considering Shakespeare's context, the general consensus of society was that witches were **preternaturally** evil. They constantly talk about their various misdeeds and almost brag about their nature, but they also allude to the fact they see a great purpose for Macbeth – a powerful destiny that would shape Scotland. Alternatively, they could also foresee the destruction caused by influencing such a man.

Preternatural: beyond what is normal or natural.

They follow Hecate's command to punish Macbeth for his arrogance, but the prophecies used to punish him and to make him afraid backfire, rendering him even more arrogant and inciting him to commit atrocities such as the murder of Macduff's family. Ultimately, their motives are left purposely vague, and that may be for the best, as the greatest unease comes from the unknown, and the witches most definitely represent that with their existential concerns of destiny and morality.

Malcolm

Son of King Duncan, and future king of Scotland, Malcolm is one of the major players in the political game that engulfs Scotland in the wake of his father's murder. Malcolm's story is one of an heir and son, unlawfully dispossessed of his rightful position as king of Scotland and accused of murdering his own father. However, Malcolm is in a sort of literary limbo with his rebellion being a crucial part of the Macbeth's downfall and the final act of the play, but not being fleshed out enough compared to Macduff, the primary foil for Macbeth. In fact, Malcolm and Macbeth only share two scenes together: when Macbeth meets with Duncan after his encounter with the witches (Act 1, Scene 4) and when the thanes, Malcolm, Donalbain, and Macbeth discover Duncan murdered (Act 2, Scene 3). There is very little relationship established between Malcolm and Macbeth, and when considering Malcolm's young age, it makes sense why Macduff was better suited to act as a foil to Macbeth rather than Malcolm. However, in the final act of the play Malcolm is partially responsible for Macbeth's downfall, as aside from leading the army, he is the one to instruct his soldiers to cover themselves in the branches of Birnam Wood to hide their march to Dunsinane castle, unwittingly fulfilling the prophecy of Macbeth's demise.

When Malcolm is introduced in the first act of the play, he is portrayed simply as a good and loyal son to his father with some position of military importance, as he not only brings the sergeant bearing news of Macbeth's victory to Duncan (Act 1, Scene 2) but is also present at meetings with his father's thanes. Other than this, it is only after his father's death in Act 2, Scene 4 that the audience gets a better sense of his personality with him displaying an incredibly mature amount of caution and foresight alongside his brother when they discuss fleeing the castle and their suspicion to who murdered Duncan, with Malcolm's quote of "let's not consort with them / to show an unfelt sorrow is an office which the false man does easy" being particularly telling, as he successfully guesses at Macbeth's fake sorrow. It is not until Act 4 when Malcolm returns, and the scene which he and Macduff have all to themselves (Act 4, Scene 3) is crucial to his character, as it adds layers unseen in the assumed good and intelligent young man.

He concocts a clever ploy to discern Macduff's true loyalties by pretending to confess to be a lustful, greedy, horrendous person, and only when Malcolm hears Macduff denounce him as unworthy does Malcolm trust that Macduff is indeed committed to the good of the land. This scene depicts Malcolm as a savvy politician – a trait Shakespeare often celebrated in potential kings and leaders in his plays. He also ascends to the throne in Act 5 without having to commit the sin of regicide himself; thus, Shakespeare implies this inherently good and clever boy will make for a wise and stable king.

The Thanes

Out of all the minor characters within the play, the thanes hold possibly the largest and most influential political roles. Their allegiance is what determines stability in Scotland, so it is worth noting when the balance shifts as their abandonment of Macbeth in the final act signals that Malcolm is the more likely victor with the country united on his side in their war. Representing the various regions of Scotland, the thanes are granted little in personality, as Macduff is the only one amongst them to adopt a major role within the play's plot.

However, we do see Ross and Lennox offer perspectives on some of Macbeth's atrocities. For instance, Ross discusses the unnatural occurrences happening in the world in the wake of Duncan's death at the end of the second act, and Lennox at the end of the third sarcastically praises Macbeth's rule so far and not only reveals the growing discontentment arising from his misrule but that Macduff has fled to England to seek Malcolm. On the most basic level, the thanes are a tool for the audience to better understand the events in the play, echoing the plot in a more compressed manner.

The Murderers

Used as basically tools by Macbeth, the murderers hold little importance in the overall story of *Macbeth*, though their actions do have great consequence as they're to kill Banquo and Lady Macduff and her child. Their use by Macbeth represents a shift in his character, as instead of doing the killing himself, like what he did with Duncan and the servants, he instead hires and manipulates these men into doing his killing for him. Whatever little honour Macbeth could justify having with his previous murders is gone by the action of hiring others to do it for him, thus removing the direct association and consequence. The murderers, from a modern understanding, may be a message about the **flawed feudal system** in place at the context of the story, as they are easily manipulated into blaming Banquo for their own misfortunes. Yet when considering the absolute monarchy Shakespeare wrote the play in, it is unlikely that was the true intent. Rather, it is clear the murderer's presence in the play is to **highlight how little Macbeth at this point cares about anyone but himself** and maintaining his power as king.

Lady Macduff

Lady Macduff, though only present for a single scene, leaves quite the impact in the brief time she is present. Strong-willed and strong-tongued, she is an example of Shakespeare writing a truly strong and good female character, as she shows nothing but care and dedication to the safety of her family. It is no wonder that Lady Macduff, much like her husband is for Macbeth, serves as a **foil to Lady Macbeth,** highlighting the dark parallels between them. Whereas Lady Macbeth is initially shown as cunning and unsatisfied with her female identity, Lady Macduff is **blunt and fiercely loyal to her role as a mother.** Lady Macbeth descends into madness near her death, unable to protect herself or her husband in the war to come, possibly giving up hope and committing suicide. Lady Macduff, dies crying out the warning for the rest of her family and household to flee, displaying one last act of bravery before her demise. It is these contrasts that lie at the heart of Lady Macduff's character and makes her murder all the more tragic, as Shakespeare – in a single scene – creates a character deep enough to elicit sympathy from his audience.

Hecate

Though we can argue about how much of the play is truly the result of supernatural interference, it is nevertheless clear what Hecate's presence represents thematically: **the absolute power of destiny and natural forces.** Hecate originally was a Greek goddess, but Shakespeare's appropriation of her in a Scottish context is justified, as even to his Christian audience, her role and name was well known. Though Hecate is an all-powerful deity, Shakespeare does not make her above human conflict and emotion however, as she demonstrates a distaste for Macbeth and his arrogance after a taste of fulfilling his destiny. As the seeming master of destiny within the play's context, Shakespeare writes her in such a way that she admonishes her servants for flaunting and granting her power to those unworthy, indicating that Hecate has either some form of morality guiding her actions or, more ominously, fears the power destiny grants to those who take it. Hecate herself, though a dark supernatural being, seems to be the judge of Macbeth and instructs her witches to grant Macbeth more prophecies in order to punish him for his hubris. It is almost as if Shakespeare is writing Hecate as the representation of the tragic justice inflicted within tragedies to their tragic heroes. Yet Macbeth is highly debated to actually be a tragic hero, so rather than serve as a figure of justice and karma, Hecate can be interpreted as an avenger and punisher of Macbeth's misdeeds. Even though embodying this seemingly just spirit, it should be reinforced that Hecate during the time of *Macbeth*'s writing was feared figure and was almost demonic in its association with witches. Once again Shakespeare demonstrates an ability to create complex characters even on the minor level.

Fleance

Though given very few lines, Fleance's role is much more significant thematically considering his direct link to prophecy within *Macbeth*. Banquo's prophecy of "thou shalt get kings, though thou be none" can be interpreted as in direct reference to Fleance, being Banquo's first and what can be assumed only son who will one day (somehow – Shakespeare leaves this ambiguous!) inherit the Scottish throne. As with all the prophecies in *Macbeth*, the interpretation that Fleance is to be king should be taken with a grain of salt, as he disappears from the play after death of his father and Malcolm becomes king of Scotland after defeating Macbeth. From an in-text context, the prophecy gives Fleance as much claim to the throne as Macbeth did when wrongly usurping Duncan. But it would defeat the purpose of the entire thematic meaning of the play if Fleance arises to the position of king using the unnatural means of prophecy after all the chaos that has been caused because of it. Instead it can be inferred that Fleance's purpose was more political and as another example of the motif between fathers and sons. To explain the political purpose behind Fleance and the probable meaning of Banquo's prophecy, it is best to link back to the context the play was written and performed in, as King James I of England was said to be descended from Banquo's and Fleance's line. By including this direct link to his linage, Shakespeare ensured the favour of his patron and king, and served to continue the absolute nature of prophecy and destiny. It should also be said that Fleance's escape, is one of the major causes of Macbeth's paranoia and the stress induced by the situation could have caused the hallucination of Banquo's ghost, if that interpretation of events is to be believed.

Siward and Young Siward

Siward and his son aren't hugely important, but are useful points of reference for Macbeth's violent cruelty in Act 5, as well as for the thematic concern of fathers and sons. Siward is King Duncan's brother and so is one of the men who join with Malcolm in taking up arms against Macbeth. He also expresses his enthusiasm for his son Young Siward to experience the battle given that he is not yet a man (i.e. a teenager). Tragically, Young Siward is killed in Act 5 Scene 7 when he bravely charges Macbeth, renouncing him as an "abhorred tyrrant." This is yet another example of Macbeth slaying a child, and as explained on page 46, another instance in which Macbeth destroys a father/son relationship by killing someone and leaving another to grieve their loss.

In spite of Young Siward's age, Ross recounts his valiant efforts to his father by saying "like a man he died." Through this, perhaps Shakespeare implies that boys like Young Siward and Macduff's son are in fact more 'manly' than Macbeth, as both children express their moral disapproval of Macbeth while defending the honour of their fathers, thereby strengthening Shakespeare's critique of the kind of gender stereotypes perpetuated by Lady Macbeth who equates masculinity with violence and cruelty.

Section 5
Key Themes Analysis

Power

Power lies at the heart of many of the characters' desires and it is the desire to gain and maintain such power that guides their actions. Yet the nature of power is complex within *Macbeth* as Shakespeare uses it himself as a tool for his tragedy, subverting its nature and expectations in ways that raise important questions from his audience. It is these questions where the heart of the analysis on power lie, with the most important ones being: what is the true power in the text, the throne or the promise of one? Who truly wields power in this world, the men who fight for it or the women who scheme? What is the true power, the physical or the supernatural?

The first question is one whose answer lies in context and history, as the story of Shakespeare's *Macbeth* is based off a real time in Scottish history in which the throne was contested for in a series of bloody wars in which kings died at the hands of their successors. Though not as drawn out and complex as the real history, Shakespeare demonstrates in the play the power the throne of Scotland holds as it opens with Duncan finally quashing a rebellion against him. The throne's power over the king is made even more apparent when Macbeth murders Duncan for even a mere promise of holding it and goes on to hunt down and kill anyone who threatens his claim to it (such as Banquo with his prophesised line of kings and the rebel thane Macduff). Yet when wins his throne, his power seems to vanish. Thanes abandon him in favour of Malcolm, and all of a sudden confusion arises to what power the throne even held in the first place.

The illusion power is a vital idea in the play, as it resonates with the motif of the known and unknown. No one within the play or in the audience truly knows where power resides. A case could be made that it is the women of *Macbeth* that are the true power players, with Lady Macbeth being the one to devise the plan to murder Duncan and convince her husband to do it, even physically getting involved with the act. Lady Macbeth adds much to this illusion of power, as the mere temptation of it corrupts her morals and leads her to grasp at something that is truly not there, doomed to madness and death. Lady Macbeth falls into the trap that is power, as true power is often wield by forces they cannot even begin to comprehend. That is where the supernatural comes in, as Shakespeare uses the witches and their prophecies to be the great catalyst for the war and tragedy to come.

This raises yet another question about the nature of power within the play, as if the witches can easily shape the whole political nature with a few simple words, then what does that say about the power a king holds? The motif of the known and unknown is at its strongest here, as from the perspective of Hecate, the seeming master of fate and prophecy, the squabbles between Macbeth, Malcolm, and Macduff must seem like a game, as she and her servants appear to be the true puppet masters controlling who reigns and who dies. Ultimately, Shakespeare reveals how desperately seeking and clinging to power is not sustainable, and characters like Macbeth and Lady Macbeth who prioritise this above all else will inevitably psychologically unravel.

Ambition

Often cited as Macbeth's fatal flaw, ambition is what many would view as the primary reason for the horrific acts that take place throughout the play. It is mostly associated with Macbeth and his wife, though a sense of ambition can also be seen in the desires of characters such as Malcolm and Macduff. Their perspective, as well Macbeth's and Lady Macbeth's, are key to understanding what Shakespeare is saying about ambition thematically in the text.

The most obvious display of the theme of ambition within the play is Macbeth himself, as whether he is a tragic hero or not, ambition seems to be a major personal flaw with his character. Initially, however, Macbeth's ambition isn't made as obvious to the audience as when faced with the possibility to take the throne through prophecy, he does not immediately act to claim it or even think murdering Duncan to take it. It is only when his wife's ambition is added to his own and he is shamed by her, with Lady Macbeth viciously quoting "when you durst do it then you were a man and to be more than what you were, you would be so much more the man." After this, though still hesitant, Macbeth decides to act upon his ambition, as Shakespeare leaves two clues to what drives Macbeth's fatal and tragic ambition. The first is his shame, as Macbeth, an already powerful man granted even more power, is outwitted and admonished by his wife whom he had probably assumed would not have begun plotting the moment she gained the information. By acting upon his wife's plan and eventually creating his own without her knowledge or consent, he rids himself of the shame of his initial hesitancy. The second driving force for his ambition is prophecy and the guarantee that comes with it, as he is at first sceptical of the witches' promise that he will be Thane of Cawdor and then king until he receives news of his new title from the thanes and Duncan. From that point onwards, Macbeth begins to commit to his ambition with the greatest example being after his second visit to the witches, as he says "from this moment the very firstlings of my heart shall be the firstlings of my hand."

The ambition of other characters in the play is less emphasised, but still important enough to warrant a brief mention. The most prominent of these minor ambitions are those of Lady Macbeth whose ambition is less clear than her husband's. Though she is the one to organise the death of Duncan and gains herself the position of Queen of Scotland, the political power it can be assumed she desired is not granted to her, as Macbeth becomes more and more distant the more his own ambition overshadows hers, driving her to guilt-ridden madness.

Malcolm's and Macduff's ambition is driven by vengeance after the deaths of their father and family respectively at the hands of Macbeth. However, their ambitions to return Scotland to a just and rightful ruler is presented as a far more righteousness endeavour, particularly as they are merely responding to the tragic events that were out of their control.

Violence

Macbeth is amongst Shakespeare's most infamously violent tragedies. Though not depicting a family destruction on the levels of *Romeo and Juliet* or *Hamlet*, Shakespeare does not flinch from display harrowing levels of violence within his play, as the various murders and wars fought do not hide its brutal nature and destructive cycle.

It is important to note that Shakespeare deliberately chooses to start and end *Macbeth* with war and rebellion. Starting with the end of rebellion against Duncan, Shakespeare uses a heavy amount of foreshadowing within the violence mentioned during the meetings between Duncan and his thanes. Firstly, the 'Thane of Cawdor', described as a strong and repentant warrior is said to have been executed, probably via beheading for treason. Macbeth himself, who would be raised to the position of 'Thane of Cawdor' before murdering Duncan to become king, is described as and shown to be a great warrior and effectively rebels against the throne by killing Duncan and usurping Malcolm, only to die in a rebellion against him and being beheaded, though not entirely repentant unlike his predecessor. Shakespeare utilises this foreshadowing and repetition to seemingly highlight the endless cycle of violence created when one does wrong to another.

Shakespeare also explores the disturbingly extreme levels of violence characters will go to in order to maintain some semblance of power. Initially, Macbeth seemingly only intends to kill Duncan and blame the servants, thus resolving the problem immediately. Yet it doesn't work as expected as Shakespeare demonstrates that **violence will always lead to more violence,** as Macbeth rashly kills the two servants to hide his guilt. This action raises suspicion amongst Banquo and Macduff, leading Macbeth to send murderers to kill them and their families. This backfires on him however, as his failure to kill Fleance means that Banquo's prophecy could still come true, and the slaughter of Macduff's family ignites a fury within Macduff, who is the only man who can kill Macbeth according to prophecy. An entire bloody civil war is started over Macbeth's use of violence, as after his first killing he becomes so numb that he orders the deaths of anyone in his castle who is afraid. This was and still is a powerful reminder by Shakespeare that violence is never the right solution and should be avoided lest a cycle is created and everything is thrown into chaos.

Destiny

From the first act to the last, the ideas of prophecy and its consequences lie at the core of *Macbeth*'s tragic nature. Portrayed as a supernatural force, Shakespeare in an understanding of his personal context treats the concept of tragedy as a sister to destiny, as many of the tragic and brutal demises of the characters within the play are predetermined by forces beyond their understanding.

The existential dread Shakespeare creates with destiny is realised perfectly through the use of the witches' prophecies and Hecate's complex motivations. When looking at the prophecies given to Banquo and Macbeth, it appears that their fulfilment has nothing supernatural surrounding it, even though they interpret it as such. Macbeth being granted the title of 'Thane of Cawdor' was established in a scene *before* they meet with the witches. Furthermore, Macbeth's rise to the throne is accomplished through his murderous acts. The second set of prophecies that decree he is invincible unless three seemingly impossible things occur are all fulfilled with Macbeth's cruel actions provoking Macduff, a man born from a caesarean birth, and Malcolm who rallies an army to avenge his father Duncan's death using the branches of Birnam Wood for camouflage. Even Banquo's prophecy, though not fulfilled, can easily be achieved without supernatural means as Macbeth set the blueprint by simply murdering the previous monarch. This theory is incredibly valid when considering the evidence presented, but the question is raised to what is the point of the theme of destiny if all the prophecies can be explained away so easily and realistically?

The answer lies in not how destiny is represented in the play but rather **what attitudes towards destiny say about characters,** particularly Macbeth. As stated above, being associated with Hecate and the witches, destiny is linked innately to darkness and even evil, so aligning oneself with these forces can be assumed to have negative impacts. That is exactly what happens as Macbeth, in contrast to Banquo's caution and patience, acts upon promises of destiny, driven by his ambition and wife's manipulation and fulfils his own prophecies to the point in which he becomes delusional and arrogant enough to think he can shape and conform it to his will and desire. This horrifically and ironically backfires on him as he ignores the seeming absolute nature of prophecy when he is proclaimed invincible until Birnam Wood comes to Dunsinane and a man not born of a woman fights and kills him. So lost in his false perception that he is the master of his fate, Macbeth fails to realise that he puts his faith in a prophecy that specifically outlines how and where he will be defeated. It is a poignant and frightening message and highlights our eternal fears about fate and destiny: **the future is unknown and can never be mastered even by the most powerful men.**

Guilt

This is perhaps the most emotionally powerful and haunting theme of the play. *Macbeth* is filled with characters suffering from the harsh nature of guilt, and guilt is often used in the text as a punishment for unjust actions. Contextually, this portrayal of guilt would have resonated well with Shakespeare's audience, as their devout Christian beliefs centre on the guilt brought about by sin and the divine consequences for those who do not repent. In the case of *Macbeth*, the theme of guilt is used to destroy characters for their wrongdoing either inspiring their redemption or driving them to madness.

Even before the murder, Macbeth felt guilty. The first hint of this complex guilt is in the first act when he is alone with himself and contemplates what killing Duncan means in his remark: "first, as I am his kinsman and subject... this Duncan hath borne his faculties so meek" before telling his wife he refuses to go ahead with the murder and to stop discussing the plan. Only when shamed does he give in to his ambition and suppress feelings of guilt for the regicide he will commit that night. Macbeth's guilt and fear of the action is visualised by his hallucination of a floating dagger and the supposed voices he heard in Duncan's chamber. His line "I am afraid to think on what I have done look on it again I dare not" is a blatant admission of guilt and the motif of blood introduced within this scene linking to the fact that guilt cannot be washed off. Yet Macbeth, even after witnessing the ghost of Banquo, seems to be able to wash off his guilt quite easily as he is able to commit numerous horrible atrocities and seems relatively remorseless until the end. He confidently states that if there were no consequences, murder would be easy and best done quickly. These are not the thoughts of a guilty man; rather, Macbeth merely fears the end to his own power.

The same cannot be said about Lady Macbeth and Macduff however, as their guilt is significantly more honest and brutal in nature. Macduff suffers guilt from the news that his family has been killed by Macbeth for his treasonous flight to Malcolm. Yet unlike Macbeth and Lady Macbeth, Shakespeare doesn't cruelly destroy Macduff, rather Macduff uses the pain caused by his guilt to exact vengeance to avenge his dead family. Much like many aspects of Macduff's character, Shakespeare uses him as a foil to Macbeth to show how guilt can be a positive motivating force as opposed to a purely selfish or self-defeating one. He does the opposite however with Lady Macbeth, as the harrowing and destructive side of guilt is inextricably tied to her character. The bold, scheming woman who proclaimed to demons and dark spirits to strip her of her femininity is transformed into a pitiful madwoman by the play's end. To make this sudden and shocking shift even clearer, Shakespeare employs the motif of blood with Lady Macbeth as she fruitlessly attempts to wash her hands clean of the blood she previous had on them. If Macbeth's punishment was for him to lose everything as king before being killed, then Lady Macbeth's is to be crushed by the weight of her greed and actions. She talks of Duncan, whose blood she had on her hands literally and metaphorically, being the architect of his death. She speaks of Lady Macduff and her family, slaughtered at the order of the man she put and pushed into power. It is no wonder that her death is most often interpreted as a suicide, as the seemingly relentless nature of the guilt taking from her sleep and sanity must have been too much to bear as her whole world collapsed.

Gender

Though not as commonly studied as the themes of ambition, power, and destiny, the role gender has on *Macbeth*'s overall messages and narrative is no less important. Contextually, Shakespeare wrote during and about a time where men and women had strict and expected roles, with men especially in high positions of political power being expected to be strong and warriors, with their lady wives raising a family. Yet Shakespeare subverts these traditional roles and instead portrays a much more complex gender landscape in which the men and women of *Macbeth* act outside of their typical contextual stereotypes, giving the text an enduring legacy in our modern world.

Lady Macbeth is the prime example of the subversion of gender in the play. Typically, Shakespeare's villains are male, with figures like Iago and Claudius serving as antagonists for their respective tragic heroes. Yet in *Macbeth*, from her first introduction in Act 1, Lady Macbeth is portrayed not only as a villain equal to her counterparts, but is also a starkly different figure than what would be assumed of a noble lady during medieval Scotland. Sharp tongued and critical, her first line immediately establishes her as a figure of power in the play: "Glamis art thou and Cawdor thou shalt be... I fear thy nature for it is too full o'th' milk of human kindness." Here, Shakespeare brilliantly develops a character seemingly in charge of her own husband's power, as she not only mocks him for his lack of ambition but single-handedly devises the plan to cruelly murder Duncan. Shakespeare thus introduces the idea of a woman desiring to be greater her station and gender would allow her to be. The most shocking example of this is her demanding spirits "unsex [her] here and make thick [her] blood," signalling her desire to change her own gender so that she can attain greater power. This is seemingly incredibly progressive from a modern perspective, but considering her pitiful downfall by play's end it is clear these words and actions were written with negative, foreshadowing intent.

Lady Macbeth isn't the only woman depicted within the play however, as Lady Macduff, Hecate, and witches all hold unique roles and influence within the play. Lady Macduff, almost as sharp tongued and disapproving of her own husband's actions, is representative of what the true noble woman should be according to Shakespeare – chiefly a strong and protective mother. Hecate is an all-powerful being, pulling the strings of destiny and punishing men like Macbeth for his arrogance. The witches dispense powerful prophecies that shape the political landscape and caused untold suffering and bloodshed. For a text dominated by the actions of a man, the women of his world seem to hold the greatest influence in retrospect. Initially, Macbeth is powerless and passive to his wife's manipulation, shut down at the mention of not going through with the plan to murder Duncan. It is curious to why Shakespeare portrays Macbeth, an incredibly powerful man and warrior known for his courage and bravery. Maybe it is to highlight the good nature Macbeth has before his dark wife corrupts him, or maybe it is to highlight how truly ambitious and powerful Lady Macbeth thinks herself within this scene.

Section 6
Structural Features Analysis

Motifs

Blood

The motif of blood is one of the most striking in play, and is associated quite blatantly with the theme of guilt. In an explicit and visual sense, Shakespeare quite literally displays blood being present on those who have committed guilty actions, specifically Macbeth, Lady Macbeth, and the murderer who kills Banquo. Yet blood, much like guilt, does not wash off easily. Macbeth ponders whether all "great Neptune's ocean wash this blood clean from my hand" after killing Duncan, and Lady Macbeth, who though she doesn't physically kill Duncan nevertheless plans his death and returns the daggers to the crime scene, physically associates herself with the crime and comes back covered in his blood. This last part is important as in her delusion towards the end of the play (Act 5, Scene 1) involves her miming washing her hands and disturbingly murmuring "out, damned spot! Out...who would have thought the old man to have had so much blood in him" before she wanders off and eventually meets her end. That Duncan "had so much blood in him" can also be interpreted as an indication of how healthy and full of life he was, making his murder all the more unnatural and tragic.

Consider how these depictions of blood would have appeared on stage – some productions choose to show Lady Macbeth's hands soaked in blood, or have a phantom dagger dangle in front of Macbeth as physical manifestations of their guilt, whereas others leave these elements as imaginary, meaning the audience watches Macbeth hallucinate a dagger or Lady Macbeth scrub a "damned spot" that only she can see, as visual indications that their minds are unravelling.

Fathers and sons

Though not as prominent as blood, the motif of fathers, sons, and heirs is important to understand, as it can lead to a better understanding of Macbeth's downfall. The father-son relationships depicted in the play are those of King Duncan and his sons Malcolm and Donalbain, Banquo and his son Fleance, Siward and his son Young Siward, and Macduff and his son. It is curious that **Macbeth kills a member of each pair** in order to gain and maintain his power and fulfil his various prophecies, with him personally murdering Duncan and Young Siward and sending murderers to kill Macduff's son and Banquo, with Fleance managing to the escape. The reasoning behind utilising such a motif is to demonstrate two things: Macbeth's insecurity of his power, and the harsh nature of prophecy. Macbeth seeks to kill fathers and sons in order to gain and consolidate his power. From a political perspective this is reasonable as by removing the heirs of those who oppose him, Macbeth effective rids himself of their resistance to his rule.

Yet Shakespeare involves a deeper motive, one supported by prophecy, as Macbeth doesn't just attempt to remove his, enemies' heirs out of political gain but in an attempt to fight destiny. Banquo's prophecy that his line will breed kings threatens Macbeth's right to rule as Macbeth ironically has no sons himself. In order to stop this, Macbeth kills the father but fails to kill the son, thus reaffirming the inescapable nature of destiny. This failure also severely backfires on him, as Malcolm, whom he ignores in his attempts on Fleance's life, rises against him and brings Macduff seeking vengeance against the death of his own son to slay Macbeth.

The known and unknown

The motif of the known and unknown is strongly represented in the play's dichotomous focus on the events of the natural and supernatural world. In the natural political world of *Macbeth*, its various characters plot their ascent to power and scheme their enemies' downfall. Macbeth and his wife plot the murder of their king and kin in the dark of night (in Act 1, Scene 5 and Act 1, Scene 7). Malcolm and Donalbain discuss plans to flee Scotland and to claim their rightful position as Scotland's rulers (Act 2, Scene 3), and Macbeth sends murderers in secret to kill Banquo and his son as they travel (Act 3, Scene 3). All these plots represent the secret nature of power in the play, and create intrigue designed to draw and entertain an audience, if context is to be considered. Shakespeare also adds another layer to this, as unbeknownst to his characters, another unnatural plot is unfolding itself beyond their comprehension. Witches snicker and talk about dark deeds and curses they commit to those they feel deserve it (Act 1, Scene 3). Prophecies are given that cause bloodshed, mayhem, and a tragic end. A goddess of magic dispenses terrible and tragic justice to those to arrogant to not take her power seriously (Act 3, Scene 5). It is these layers of understanding and misunderstanding that add to the drama and prestige of the text, as Shakespeare manages to expertly weave human and supernatural struggles into a coherent and gripping story expressing themes relevant to our times today.

Literary form and aesthetic features

Aside from studying the play's thematic and character aspects, analysing *Macbeth* for its structural form is just as important. Shakespeare wrote *Macbeth* in a specific way, for a specific purpose, and by understanding his authorial intent and construction of the play, we can gain a deeper understanding of the text's thematic elements.

Structure

Structurally, the play is very similar to many of Shakespeare's other tragedies. It contains five acts, broken down into scenes of varying amount and length. The placement of events and characters within these acts is deliberate as Shakespeare follows a very specific formula in structuring his tragedies in order to present and gain the most out of the drama he writes and his audience's response. In the case of *Macbeth*, this structure will be broken down using reference to the various scenes of the play itself with deviations to the formula being pointed out when they appear.

Act 1 of Shakespeare's tragedies is pure establishment and centres on introducing its major characters, themes, and plot with scene one of such an act not involving the text's subject, rather side characters helping to introduce the audience to what the play is about literally and thematically. In the case of *Macbeth* all these aspects are present, as the first act centres on Macbeth's meeting with the witches, learning of his prophecies, and the plotting between him and his wife to kill Duncan. Shakespeare establishes his major themes of destiny, power, and ambition through the various conversations and monologues in this act, and the thunderous opening with the witches establishes the dark and supernatural tone that hangs over the play until its end.

Acts 2 and 3 can grouped together in the tragic formula as they represent that cause and effect of the characters' actions (with Act 2 being the causes and Act 3 the effects). The causes, such as Duncan's murder, Malcolm's flight, and Macbeth's ascension as king, all happen within the Act 2 as the effects are felt throughout Act 3 with Macduff fleeing Scotland, the murder of Banquo, and Macbeth beginning his descent into madness witnessing the ghost of Banquo. Act 3 itself represents the play's first climax and is usually the pinnacle of the drama and action until the second and final climax in Act 5, yet it is here where *Macbeth* differs from Shakespeare's other tragedies. In order to sustain the eerie atmosphere of the play, Shakespeare sprinkles in quiet and unsettling scenes of self-reflection and discussion raising themes of guilt, gender, and violence throughout these acts. Whether it is Macbeth pondering if he can ever wash Duncan's blood off (Act 2, Scene 2), or Ross talking about the unnatural occurrences in the world since Duncan was murdered (Act 2, Scene 4), or Hecate plotting Macbeth's downfall (Act 3, Scene 5), Shakespeare never breaks the creeping tension present in the play.

Act 4 probably differs from convention the most, as instead of serving as the typical respite and second round of plotting, much of it is devoted to action and intense moments. Still establishing the conflict in scenes like Macbeth's second meeting with the witches (Act 4, Scene 1) and Malcolm and Macduff's passionate political discussion (Act 4, Scene 3), much of the act is grand in its nature. Macbeth's prophecies of his supposed invincibility and supernatural ways that it can be broken and Lady Macduff's brutal murder are all significant events that serve to show the consequences of the themes raised in earlier scenes, and much depth and development is granted to the characters in this act, specifically Malcolm and Macduff, whose role in Act 5 is well established here.

Act 5 is final climax and much like the rest of Shakespeare's tragedies involves a large amount of action and the culmination of the foreshadowing throughout the play. Macbeth and Malcolm go to war, as the consequences of his crimes and his fight against destiny tragically destroy him. Lady Macbeth driven insane sleepwalks while confessing her crimes before dying, while Macbeth ponders on the futility of life and destiny in his "tomorrow" soliloquy before falling to his foil Macduff. Act 5 is the end and serves as Shakespeare's chance to convey lessons to the audience, usually with a speech by the last and most pure survivor (in this case Malcolm).

Tragedy

Macbeth as with many of Shakespeare's other tragedies, is based of Aristotle's tragic theory. Tragedy to Aristotle was "purgative" and designed to act as *pathos* for the audience, allowing them to realise their worst aspects from watching the play and freeing (purging) them from their being once the lesson is learned, reaching *catharsis*. Aristotle also believed that the hero the tragedy must be flawed and such a flaw should cause *hubris*, and it is often only through death that a hero can redeem themselves.

Macbeth, though mainly a tragedy, handles its characters very differently than Aristotle's method would allow. Rather than create one-dimensional melodramatic characters, Shakespeare adds layers of ambiguity and fallibility. Macbeth himself can be seen as either a tragic hero or an irredeemable villain. However, Macduff's story fits the Aristotelian mould nearly perfectly, as he suffers due to his tragic flaw, sacrificing his family for his loyalty to Scotland, and eventually redeems himself by the play's end, setting everything right by killing Macbeth and placing Malcolm on the throne in his stead. The only difference is that Macduff does not die, rather he lives on and can be assumed at peace by avenging his family. Has Macduff reached true catharsis? To Aristotle, this meant a personal and emotional discovery, in contrast to vengeance that was merely based on reaction and desire. Mentally, the audience never gets to know what Macduff feels after Macbeth's death or if he is at peace with his family's death, and so the extent to which the text can be interpreted as true Aristotelean tragedy is left somewhat ambivalent.

Though there are significant examples of it throughout the text, the more likely explanation is that Shakespeare uses this tragic structure and subverts it for his own socio-cultural purpose. Shakespeare's world was a religious one, shaped by ideas of divine penance and punishment. Though his characters embody the tragic struggle between freedom and destiny, the heavy use of religious imagery and the association of destiny with supernatural even demonic forces leads the tragedy to be somewhat diluted from its original intention. Macbeth's and his wife's end, though tragic in their own ways, seem more like justice by the end of the play, as Macbeth is executed by Macduff – a common punishment for treason in the play's context – rather than taking his own life like the tragic heroes. Macbeth himself seems mock this traditional aspect of tragic heroes, as he infamously quotes before fighting Macduff, "why should I play the Roman fool and die on my own sword?" Hence, while some elements of Aristotle's methods are present, due to Shakespeare's and the story's original context, the tragedy is less melodramatic and more human, as the battles for vengeance and destiny are ones fought by the ordinary people.

Verse and meter

The majority of the play is written in **iambic pentameter,** which is Shakespeare's standard form of verse. This involves lines that are 10 syllables long, with stress placed on every second syllable. For instance:

> QUOTES :
> Macbeth: "So FOUL and FAIR a DAY I HAVE not SEEN."

This gives lines a sense of rhythm and flow, but it can also be used to show dynamics between characters when syllables are split between them. For example, consider this line of 10 syllables shared by Macbeth and Lady Macbeth:

> QUOTES :
> Lady Macbeth: "...And dashed the brains out, had I so sworn as you
> **Have done to this."**
>
> Macbeth: **"If we should fail—"**
>
> Lady Macbeth: **"We fail?**
> But screw your courage to the sticking place
> And we'll not fail."

Here, Macbeth attempts to interrupt his wife's horrifying efforts to convince Macbeth to make good on his promises (with her stating that she would happily murder her own child if she promised Macbeth to do so!) but his interjection of "If we should fail—" is cut off by Lady Macbeth refusing to even acknowledge the possibility. Structurally, Macbeth's doubts are being overwhelmed by Lady Macbeth's encouragement with her words surrounding him on all sides. Although analysing verse and meter can be tricky, look out for opportunities like this to comment on how Shakespeare's language may hint at other thematic ideas.

The other useful thing to talk about in terms of verse is when and why Shakespeare sometimes departs from iambic pentameter. The most notable examples of this are the witches who instead speak in **trochaic tetrameter,** meaning that there are 8 syllables per line with stress on the first syllable instead of the second:

> QUOTES :
> The Witches: "DOUble, DOUble, TOIL and TROUble,
> FIre BURN and CAULdron BUbble."

You don't have to memorise the complexities of syllable stress (and there are lines that break these rules, especially since modern pronunciation differs slightly from Jacobean England) but the important thing to note is that **the witches' dialogue is structurally opposite to that of the human characters.** The fact that they place stress differently and that their lines are shorter makes them stand out as weird and unnatural, amplifying the gap between the natural and supernatural realms, and perhaps also showcasing why the two are incompatible.

The other major instance of verse breaking down is show in Lady Macbeth in Act 5. In her psychologically unravelled state, she can no longer speak in meter (as was traditionally expected by Shakespeare's royal and noble characters) and instead only speaks in **prose** (i.e. normal English with no syllable or stress rules). This demonstrates how corrupted her mind has become as a result of her role as an accessory to regicide.

Dramatic irony

Dramatic irony is where the audience understands certain information that other characters do not. *Macbeth* is rife with this, especially surrounding the murder of Duncan. We are well aware of Lady Macbeth and Macbeth's scheming and eventual crime of regicide, meanwhile Duncan is happily arriving at their castle declaring that "this castle hath a pleasant seat" with sweet and delicate air. Even Duncan noting that the previous Thane of Cawdor was "a gentleman on whom I built an absolute trust" can be seen as dramatically ironic given that Macbeth then claims the title before also betraying Duncan.

Later, when his body is discovered, Lady Macbeth feigns shock and horror. Macbeth tells her "our royal master's murdered," to which Lady Macbeth responds "Woe, alas! What, in our house?" Thus, we witness the couple performing for the sake of their other guests like Banquo and Macduff, all while we know they are the guilty parties. Through this, Shakespeare not only enthrals the audience but also reveals to them the true, sinister nature of the Macbeths in conspiring to commit evil deeds and then mislead or blame others for their own advantage.

Imagery

Much of the imagery in *Macbeth* stems from the supernatural elements and portrayal of the witches as bearded, hideous hags who bring with them "foul and filthy air." However, there are also several instances of natural imagery being corrupted and subverted, particularly with the motif of dead or sick animals. For instance, Lady Macbeth hears a "hoarse" raven that "croaks the fatal entrance of Duncan," which is an example of auditory imagery. In Act 2, Scene 4, Ross meets with an Old Man who tells a story about how on the night of Duncan's murder, an owl kills a falcon, and Duncan's horses broke out of their stalls and ate each other. In all of these instances, the horrifying imagery mirrors the horror of what has occurred – Macbeth's killing of Duncan and subsequent murdering of innocents contaminates the kingdom, and it is only when Macbeth is killed and a righteous king claims the throne that order can be restored.

Section 7

Quote Bank

Power

Quote	Character	Act/Scene
"All hail, Macbeth, thou shalt be king hereafter!"	The Witches	Act 1, Scene 3
"Thou shalt get kings, though thou be none./ So all hail, Macbeth and Banquo!"	The Witches	Act 1, Scene 3
"New honours come upon him, / Like our strange garments, cleave not to their mould, / But with the aid of use."	Banquo	Act 1, Scene 3
"Besides, this Duncan / Hath borne his faculties so meek, hath been / So clear in his great office, that his virtues / Will plead like angels, trumpet-tongued, against / The deep damnation of his taking-off"	Macbeth	Act 1, Scene 7
"I dare do all that may become a man; / Who dares do more is none."	Macbeth	Act 1, Scene 7
"And though I could / With barefaced power sweep him from my sight / And bid my will avouch it, yet I must not, / For certain friends that are both his and mine, / Whose loves I may not drop, but wail his fall."	Macbeth	Act 3, Scene 1
"When our actions do not, / Our fears make us traitors."	Lady Macbeth	Act 4, Scene 2

Ambition

Quote	Character	Act/Scene
"This supernatural soliciting / Cannot be ill, cannot be good. If ill, / Why hath it given me earnest of success, Commencing in a truth?"	Macbeth	Act 1, Scene 3
"The Prince of Cumberland! That is a step / On which I must fall down, or else o'erleap, / For in my way it lies. Stars, hide your fires; / Let not light see my black and deep desires. / The eye wink at the hand; yet let that be / Which the eye fears, when it is done, to see."	Macbeth	Act 1, Scene 4
"Glamis thou art, and Cawdor, and shalt be / What thou art promised. Yet do I fear thy nature; / It is too full o' th' milk of human kindness / To catch the nearest way."	Lady Macbeth	Act 1, Scene 5
"Thou wouldst be great, / Art not without ambition, but without / The illness should attend it."	Lady Macbeth	Act 1, Scene 5
"That I may pour my spirits in thine ear / And chastise with the valor of my tongue / All that impedes thee from the golden round"	Macbeth	Act 1, Scene 5
"To alter favour ever is to fear. / Leave all the rest to me."	Lady Macbeth	Act 1, Scene 5
"I have no spur / To prick the sides of my intent, but only / Vaulting ambition, which o'erleaps itself / And falls on the other"	Macbeth	Act 1, Scene 7
"I go, and it is done. The bell invites me. / Hear it not, Duncan, for it is a knell / That summons thee to heaven or to hell."	Macbeth	Act 2, Scene 1
"Gainst nature still! Thriftless ambition, that will ravin up Thine own lives' means! Then 'tis most like The sovereignty will fall upon Macbeth."	Macbeth	Act 2, Scene 4
"Thou hast it now – king, Cawdor, Glamis, all, / As the weird women promised, and I fear / Thou played'st most foully for't."	Banquo	Act 3, Scene 1

Violence

Quote	Character	Act/Scene
"Unsex me here, / And fill me from the crown to the toe top-full / Of direst cruelty. Make thick my blood. Stop up th' access and passage to remorse."	Lady Macbeth	Act 1, Scene 5
"Is this a dagger which I see before me, / The handle toward my hand? Come, let me clutch thee: / I have thee not, and yet I see thee still."	Macbeth	Act 2, Scene 1
"I had laid their daggers ready; / He could not miss 'em. Had he not resembled / My fater as he slept, I had done't."	Lady Macbeth	Act 2, Scene 2
"Here lay Duncan, / His silver skin laced with his golden blood, / And his gashed stabs looked like a breach in nature."	Macbeth	Act 2, Scene 3
"Tis unnatural, / Even like the deed that's done. On Tuesday last, / A falcon [...] Was by a mousing owl hawk'd at, and kill'd."	Old Man	Act 2, Scene 4
"O horror, horror, horror! / Tonge nor heart cannot conceive nor name thee!"	Macduff	Act 2, Scene 4
"Blood will have blood"	Macbeth	Act 3, Scene 4
"I am in blood Stepped in so far that, should I wade no more, Returning were as tedious as go o'er."	Macbeth	Act 3, Scene 4
"From this moment / The very firstlings of my heart shall be / The firstlings of my hand. And even now, / To crown my thoughts with acts, be it thought and done"	Macbeth	Act 4, Scene 1
"The castle of Macduff I will surprise, / Seize upon Fife, give to th' edge o' th' sword / His wife, his babes, and all unfortunate souls / That trace him in his line."	Macbeth	Act 4, Scene 1
"What, all my pretty chickens, and their dam, / At one fell swoop?"	Macduff	Act 4, Scene 3
"Those clamorous harbingers of blood and death."	Macduff	Act 5, Scene 6

Destiny

Quote	Character	Act/Scene
"Fair is foul and foul is fair."	The Witches	Act 1, Scene 1
"For brave Macbeth (well he deserves that name), / Disdaining Fortune, with his brandished steel"	Captain	Act 1, Scene 2
"All hail Macbeth, that shalt be king herearfter."	The Witches	Act 1, Scene 3
"Lesser than Macbeth and greater... thou shalt get kings but thou be none"	The Witches	Act 1, Scene 3
"If you can look into the seeds of time, / And say which grain will grow and which will not, / Speak, then"	Banquo	Act 1, Scene 3
"If chance will have be King, why / Chance may crown me, / Without my stir."	Macbeth	Act 1, Scene 3
"I am Thane of Cawdor. If good, / Why do I yield to that suggestion / Whose horrid image doth unfix my hair / And make my seated heart knock at my ribs."	Macbeth	Act 1, Scene 3
"If't be so, / For Banquo's issue have I filed my mind, / For them the gracious Duncan have I murdered, / Put rancors in the vessel of my peace / Only for them, and mine eternal jewel / Given to the common enemy of man, / To make them kings, the seed of Banquo kings. / Rather than so, come fate into the list, / And champion me to th' utterance!"	Macbeth	Act 3, Scene 1
"Beware Macduff... The power of man, for none of woman born shall harm Macbeth... Macbeth shall never be vanquished until Great Birnam Wood to high Dunsinane hill shall come against him"	The Witches	Act 4, Scene 1

Quote	Character	Act/Scene
"She should have died hereafter; / There would have been a time for such a word. / Tomorrow and tomorrow and tomorrow, / Creeps in this petty pace from day to day / To the last syllable of recorded time / And all our yesterdays have lighted fools / The way to dusty death. Out, out, brief candle! / Life's but a walking shadow, a poor player / That struts and frets his hour upon the stage / And then is heard no more. It is a tale / Told by an idiot, full of sound and fury, / Signifying nothing."	Macbeth	Act 5, Scene 5
"Either thou, Macbeth, Or else my sword, with an unbattered edge, I sheathe again undeeded. There thou shouldst be; By this great clatter, one of greatest note Seems bruited. Let me find him, Fortune, And more I beg not."	Macduff	Act 5, Scene 6

Guilt

Quote	Character	Act/Scene
"Your face, my thane, is as a book where men / May read strange matters [...] Look like th/ innocent flower, / But be the serpent under 't."	Lady Macbeth	Act 1, Scene 5
"If it were done, when 'tis done, then 'twere well it were done quickly"	Macbeth	Act 1, Scene 7
"False face must hide what the false heart doth know."	Macbeth	Act 1, Scene 7
"Whence is that knocking? – / How is't with me, when every noise appals me? / What hands are here! Ha, they pluck out mine eyes."	Macbeth	Act 2, Scene 2
"Will all great Neptune's ocean wash this blood / Clean from my hand? No, this my hand will rather / The multitudinous seas incarnadine"	Macbeth	Act 2, Scene 2
"Methought I heard a voice cry, 'Sleep no more! / Macbeth does murder sleep: the innocent sleep'."	Macbeth	Act 2, Scene 2
"I am afraid to think on what I have done; Look on 't again I dare not"	Macbeth	Act 2, Scene 2

Quote	Character	Act/Scene
"Who can be wise, amazed, temp'rate, and furious, / Loyal and neutral, in a moment? No man. / Th'expedition of my violent love / Outrun the pauser, reason."	Macbeth	Act 2, Scene 3
"There's daggers in men's smiles"	Donalbain	Act 2, Scene 3
"O bed, to bed. There's knocking at the gate. Come, come, come, come, give me your hand. What's done cannot be undone. To bed, to bed, to bed."	Lady Macbeth	Act 5, Scene 1
"Out damned spot! Out!...who would have thought the old man to have had so much blood in him?"	Lady Macbeth	Act 5, Scene 1
"All the perfumes of Arabia will not sweeten this little hand."	Lady Macbeth	Act 5, Scene 1
"What's done cannot be undone."	Lady Macbeth	Act 5, Scene 1
"The Thane of Fife had a wife. Where is she now?...will these hands never be clean"	Lady Macbeth	Act 5, Scene 1

Gender

Quote	Character	Act/Scene
"You should be women, / And yet your beards forbid me to interpret / That you are so."	Macbeth	Act 1, Scene 3
"My thought, whose murder yet is but fantastical, / Shakes so my single state of man"	Macbeth	Act 1, Scene 3
"Come, you spirits / That tend on mortal thoughts, unsex me here"	Lady Macbeth	Act 1, Scene 5
"Fill me from the crown to the toe top-full / Of direst cruelty. Make thick my blood. / Stop up th' access and passage to remorse, / That no compunctious visitings of nature / Shake my fell purpose, nor keep peace between / Th' effect and it."	Lady Macbeth	Act 1, Scene 5
"Come to my woman's breasts, / And take my milk for gall, you murd'ring ministers"	Lady Macbeth	Act 1, Scene 5

Quote	Character	Act/Scene
"Come, thick night, / And pall thee in the dunnest smoke of hell, / That my keen knife see not the wound it makes, / Nor heaven peep through the blanket of the dark, / To cry "Hold, hold!""	Lady Macbeth	Act 1, Scene 5
"I have given such, and know / How tender 'tis to love the babe that milks me. / I would, while it was smiling in my face, / Have plucked my nipple from his boneless gums / And dashed the brains out, had I so sworn as you have done to this."	Lady Macbeth	Act 1, Scene 7
"O gentle lady, / 'Tis not for you to hear what I can speak. / The repetition in a woman's ear / Would murder as it fell."	Macduff	Act 2, Scene 3
"Are you a man?"	Lady Macbeth	Act 3, Scene 4

Supernatural

Quote	Character	Act/Scene
"When shall we three meet again? / In thunder, lightning, or in rain?"	The Witches	Act 1, Scene 1
"When the hurly-burly's done, / When the battle's lost and won."	The Witches	Act 1, Scene 1
"Fair is foul, and foul is fair; / Hover through the fog and filthy air."	The Witches	Act 1, Scene 1
"The Weird Sisters, hand in hand, / Posters of the sea and land, / Thus do go about, about"	The Witches	Act 1, Scene 3
"So foul and fair a day I have not seen."	Macbeth	Act 1, Scene 3
"That look not like th' inhabitants o' th' Earth / And yet are on 't? Live you? Or are you aught / That man may question?"	Banquo	Act 1, Scene 3
"Are you fantastical, or that indeed / Which outwardly you show?"	Banquo	Act 1, Scene 3
"Say from whence / You owe this strange intelligence or why / Upon this blasted heath you stop our way / With such prophetic greeting."	Macbeth	Act 1, Scene 3

Quote	Character	Location
"The earth has bubbles, and the water has, / And these are of them. Whither are they vanished?"	Banquo	Act 1, Scene 3
"A dagger of the mind, a false creation / Proceeding from the heat-oppressed brain? / I see thee yet, in form as palpable / As this which now I draw."	Macbeth	Act 2, Scene 1
"There's comfort yet; they are assailable [...] ere to black Hecate's summons [...] there shall be done / A deed of dreadful note."	Macbeth	Act 3, Scene 2
"Have I not reason, beldams as you are? / Saucy and overbold, how did you dare / To trade and traffic with Macbeth / In riddles and affairs of death"	Hecate	Act 3, Scene 5
"And which is worse, all you have done / Hath been but for a wayward son, / Spiteful and wrathful, who, as others do, / Loves for his own ends, not for you."	Hecate	Act 3, Scene 5
"Double, double toil and trouble; / Fire burn, and cauldron bubble"	The Witches	Act 4, Scene 1
"Show his eyes and grieve his heart. / Come like shadows; so depart."	The Witches	Act 4, Scene 1
"Thou art too like the spirit of Banquo. Down! / Thy crown does sear mine eyeballs. And thy hair, / Thou other gold-bound brow, is like the first. / A third is like the former. Filthy hags, / Why do you show me this?"	Macbeth	Act 4, Scene 1
"Infected be the air whereon they ride, / And damned all those that trust them!"	Macbeth	Act 4, Scene 1

Section 8

Sample Essays

Essay One

QUESTION: Is *Macbeth* a moral play, and is justice truly served at its end?

ESSAY	COMMENTS
INTRODUCTION *Macbeth* is among Shakespeare's most emotionally and thematically complex plays. Containing characters of grey morality and nuanced themes and ideas, the morality of *Macbeth* is remarkably unclear.[1] Though explicitly a tragedy, the text is driven more so by the emotions and desires of its characters rather than an unambiguous sense of right or wrong. Whether it is Malcolm's unusual motives and behaviour, Macduff's desire for vengeance, or the witches' and Hecate's questionably 'moral' punishment of Macbeth, Shakespeare's play offers audiences an array of dubious moral quandaries[2] in order to explore the notion of justice.	1. Remember that you don't have to be incredibly definitive about the play's meaning and messages. It's okay to just confidently state that the text is complex, and the discuss that complexity. The assessors don't want you to write sentences about what Shakespeare *definitely* intended, because we can't be sure! All you need to do is dissect the text and examine its ideas. 2. Here, we're using the introduction to open up the discussion rather than definitively answer the prompt – this can be useful if you aren't entirely sure where your discussion will take you, or if you generally prefer to leave your summative judgement for your conclusion.

PARAGRAPH 1

One of the most overlooked characters, Malcolm[3] is often associated with the good and moral side of the play, avenging his father and reclaiming Scotland. On first glance, Malcolm shows few signs of moral complexity, as he is a seemingly good son and loyal subject. However, Malcolm and his brother are forced to flee Scotland after their father is murdered and they are blamed for his death. This choice to flee is curious, as Malcolm would have had the support and protection of thanes loyal to his father, especially Macduff. Instead, Shakespeare reveals him to be a character who prioritises his own safety over the benefit of the realm, as he leaves Scotland in the hands of the tyrannical Macbeth.[4] Malcolm's questionable caution can also be seen in Act 4, Scene 3, when he seemingly manipulates Macduff into confirming his loyalty to him and his father rather than being a spy for Macbeth. Though it can be interpreted as true self-doubt, it is suspicious considering that the man who previously stated "Macbeth is as pure of snow compared to my confine less hard... Better Macbeth than such an one to reign" conveniently reveals to Macduff after an outburst of his loyalty and love for Duncan his father, that he already has an English army ten thousand men strong. We can also call into question Malcolm's motives for retaking Scotland as being born out of self-protection and selfishly claiming what he believes is rightfully his, as opposed to true patriotism and a desire to see his country liberated. Hence, Shakespeare encourages[5] audiences to more deeply examine the complex political manoeuvrings of *Macbeth,* as even amongst secondary characters we observe deception, duplicity, and dissembling.

3. Referencing more minor characters (compared to Macbeth and Lady Macbeth), though risky, is a good way to differentiate yourself from other students and shows the marker you understand the play well!

4. This is quite a sophisticated unpacking of Malcolm's significance as a character.

5. You should always aim to end your paragraphs with an authorial intent comment like this. Use Shakespeare's name and some kind of verb to describe what he is accomplishing – this will also ensure your paragraph doesn't just sound like a summary of the plot.

PARAGRAPH 2

Furthermore, Shakespeare also explores the manifold[6] nature of justice in Macduff's moral dilemma, as his struggle between country and family is amongst the most powerful and tragic in the whole play.[7] Effectively committing treason by fleeing Scotland to collaborate with Malcolm, it appears that he selfishly leaves his family behind in severe danger of the wrath of mad and proven violent Macbeth. Lady Macduff, his own wife, says as much, stating "wisdom? To leave his wife, to leave his babes in a place from whence himself does fly? He loves us not." Lady Macduff's fears are shown to be well founded as at this point in the play Macduff's reasons for his flight are not made clear and it appears he simply fled Macbeth's rule. Such an action has dire consequences however, as Shakespeare demonstrates in a visceral act of violence when Macduff's young son and wife are slain. Macduff, prior to learning of their deaths,[8] justifies leaving his family for a desire to see his country and people free. Though it drives him to support Malcolm fully and unknowingly fulfil the prophecy to kill Macbeth, Macduff's commitment to "bring thou this fiend of Scotland and myself within my sword's length set him" is somewhat disturbing considering Macduff is morally seemingly just as responsibly for the tragedy that has befallen him, even though Macbeth ordered their killing. Thus,[9] Shakespeare reveals to audiences the moral ambiguities of even the seemingly just and sympathetic characters' actions.

6. This is a great word to use when answering essay questions about moral ambiguities, or complex things like justice.

7. This topic sentence does a really good job at outlining the discussion that is to come – by the time the marker finishes this sentence, they know how this discussion links to the previous one, the primary character that we'll be drawing our evidence from, and the core thematic concern that we will be unpacking!

8. Contextualising evidence by explaining when it occurs (and what happens before or after it) is another great way to showcase your knowledge of the play.

9. Don't neglect your concluding sentences – this is your chance to explain to your assessor what your main idea is. If you make your point clearly here, your whole paragraph seems stronger. If you don't convey an argument or interpretation in the final line, then it feels like the discussion hasn't gone anywhere.

PARAGRAPH 3

Finally, Shakespeare also evinces the role of morality in relation to the witches and Hecate. Due to Shakespeare's highly superstitious and Christian context, these supernatural beings of immense and feared power are meant to be interpreted as evil. Yet together they discuss concepts of morality and see it as their role to dispense justice on those who have wronged them. In the first act, one of the witches tells a story of how she came across a sailor's wife eating chestnuts and asked for one to eat.[10] When refused and told to go away, the witch as punishment for the woman's greed and insult decides to "drain him dry as hay and he shall dwindle." Though rudely insulted, the moral 'justice' enforced by the witch is horrific and malicious in nature. This highlights[11] the twisted view Shakespeare has of morality when using these characters as they appear to take it and twist it horrifically in ways that deal pain and suffering rather than just punishment. A greater example of this is their master Hecate's desire to punish Macbeth for his arrogance after becoming king due to prophecy. Hecate predicts that Macbeth "shall spurn fate, scorn death and bear his hopes above wisdom, grace and fear," ordering her witches to grant Macbeth more prophecies that will eventually lead to his dark and violent end. On first glance, this appears to be moral,[12] as Macbeth's ambition-driven hubris has led him to take power unlawfully and murder. Yet when considering the impact of Macbeth hearing his second set of prophecies it appears that rather than just punish Macbeth, Hecate punishes all of Scotland.

10. This might seem like minor evidence, but even quotes like this can be used to support your overall argument!

11. After recounting this moment from the text, remember to explain the significance of this evidence to your marker to ensure they know what to give you credit for.

12. Remember that not every example will have a straightforward, unambiguously 'correct' interpretation, however. You can also unpack potential alternate views, and examine the complexity of the play by pointing out that sometimes, we can interpret things in different ways.

Lady Macduff and her whole family are slain due to the witches' warning of Macduff, many die in a war fought for a throne, and Lady Macbeth is driven into a suicidal insanity due to the guilt of her and husband's actions to take the throne.[13] Rather than simply and morally let Macbeth create his own downfall, Hecate in some form of self-justified morality accelerates and exacerbates the situation causing a huge amount of unnecessary suffering in the process. To this end, Shakespeare presents audiences with a complex portrait of moral justice, and shows that true evil and tragedy cannot be attributed to any one character or force.

CONCLUSION

Ultimately, the morality of *Macbeth* is as multifaceted as its characters. Questions of who is right or justified are fraught with contextual implications, but in essence, the play invites audiences to be more critical about what is just, presenting us with an outcome tinged with both retribution and regret.[14]

13. This is a good summation of the tragic elements of the text.

14. Though your conclusion can be quite short, always ensure you take the discussion back to the core of the prompt, and answer the question directly.

Essay Two

QUESTION: To what extent do the themes, characters, and ideas present within Shakespeare's *Macbeth* carry enduring relevance to today's context?

ESSAY	COMMENTS
INTRODUCTION Shakespeare's tragedies, though incredibly unique, still carry relevance to the modern era despite being over four centuries old. Whether it is the various fatal flaws in his characters or the heavily themed, intricate, and ultimately tragic plots, Shakespeare's texts are steeped in integrity, evoking audience's interests across continents and generations.[1] One his most important and poignant is *Macbeth*,[2] whose complex and tragic characters represent themes of power, ambition, guilt, violence, and power still relevant to today's context. **PARAGRAPH 1** *Macbeth* presents situations in which the nature of power is confused and the struggle for it violent and destructive. Throughout the text, various characters are given promises of power and such promise leads to their corruption and eventually cruel demise. Macbeth, the central character and arguably antagonist, is granted a supernatural prophecy that he will become Thane of Cawdor and then "king herafter."[3]	1. This is a more general introduction to suit the broader scope of this prompt. 2. Always make sure you distinguish between *Macbeth* the play and Macbeth the character (either by italicising, underlining, or putting single quote marks around the play's title). 3. Try to keep your quotes short and sweet. This kind of precision makes it even easier for your assessor to give you marks!

This initial prophecy is what sends the tragedy into motion, as lured by the promise of power via his own internal ambition, Macbeth finds himself committing horrible actions in order to wield and maintain the power seemingly destined for him. Macbeth's murder of Duncan is objectively a wrong action, and is obviously wrong by today's standards – even to Shakespeare's contemporary audience[4] this blatant example of the corruption of power would have been harrowing. Contextually, under the rule of King James I, Shakespeare's audience would have been familiar with the corruption power brought as very similar to Macbeth's assassination, there was an attempted assassination and usurpation of King James I. Known as the infamous Gunpowder Plot,[5] Shakespeare took obvious inspiration from that and the real history, as the real king Macbeth slew the real king Duncan in order to become high king of Scotland, displaying the relevancy of the themes of power present in the play.[6]

PARAGRAPH 2
Outside of power and the struggles it brings, *Macbeth* puts forth other topics relevant to a modern context,[7] one of the most interesting of which being gender. Shakespeare, seemingly going against his context's view on the role of women, presents a complex range of ideas and perspectives from the point of view of the women in his text. The most obvious of these is Lady Macbeth's arc, in which she desires power significantly more than her husband and manipulates him to raise their social standing, elevating her to the status of a queen.

4. I'd also recommend talking about both modern and historical audiences, as this adds more sophistication to your argument.
5. Context is an important part of all Shakespearean texts and should have a place in your essay.
6. This paragraph ends with an incisive remark about authorial intent, and the overarching message of the play – it's a good idea to learn a handful of these broad interpretations that you can apply to multiple essay questions and themes.
7. This is an effective linking sentence to bridge the gap between one paragraph and the next, all while ensuring a sustained focus on the prompt.

Contextually, even in a male-driven society, queens could still wield immense political power, with Queen Elizabeth I being a long-time patron of Shakespeare and an incredibly powerful monarch. Yet Shakespeare goes further and addresses a topic incredibly relevant to modern times with Lady Macbeth and the other female characters of the play, and that is dissatisfaction with their role and rights within society. Lady Macbeth makes this palpable in her infamous "unsex me spirits" declaration, while Lady Macduff admonishes the foolishness of her husband's exile from Scotland and grows angry at her lack of knowledge of why, harshly responding to someone telling her to be patient for her husband with the line "patience... he had none. His flight was madness."[8] Yet the extent of this female representation goes further as the use of the witches and Hecate as the commanders of destiny, though they can be interpreted as evil, wield immense power for females[9] and seemingly punish Macbeth for his arrogance and lead him to his downfall through prophecy. Thus, Shakespeare's exploration of the boundaries of gender expectations remains a resonant message for modern audiences.

PARAGRAPH 3
In addition, the play also conveys to its audience the transcendent[10] message that violence only begets more violence. Shakespeare depicts how self-destructive small acts of violence can be to the character of a person.

8. This paragraph displays a highly adept integration of quotes and evidence from across the text, blending them with analysis in a very fluent way.
9. Linking separate themes and ideas together is a crucial at writing at a highly level and shows the marker a deep understanding of the text.
10. This is a good word to use when commenting on the play's textual integrity.

To use Macbeth as an example, a seemingly good man at the beginning of the text is twisted into a violent and murderous tyrant by its end. Initially hesitant, Macbeth eventually succumbs to his own dark ambitions and kills Duncan, beginning a cycle of violence. This act then requires Macbeth to continue killing to hide his secret and to maintain his position as king, including his murder of the servants and ordered killing of Banquo. Moreover, he incites others to want to commit violence against him,[11] such as Malcolm and Macduff, as a consequence. This cycle of murder and war only gets bigger and bigger as Macbeth is seemingly consumed by violence and darkly demonstrates the callousness that is an irrevocable part of society and humanity. Macbeth's trajectory takes him from a man hesitating to commit one murder in Act 1 to a person who promotes the order "hang those who talk of fear" in Act 5, referring to innocent civilians afraid of the war he created. Shakespeare raises a powerful message here and one that remains relevant to any society that is plagued by violence and fallibility.

11. Here, we have a great dissection of the cyclical nature of violence and death in the play. Remember that there are two core parts of this vicious cycle: Macbeth must commit more and more murders, and his increasingly violent actions compel other characters to act violently as well.

CONCLUSION

To say that *Macbeth* is somewhat relevant to a modern context is a severe understatement. The messages and themes that the text's characters represent are incredibly relevant and express a number of versatile ideas and commentaries on modern society's issues. Ultimately,[12] Shakespeare's composition of *Macbeth* serves as a testament to the enduring traits of humanity, both good and bad, and acts as a stark reminder of what we are capable of.

12. Make sure your conclusion is effective and concise. It is the last thing that the market will read, so you should endeavour to 'zoom out' and make interpretive comments about the text as a whole.

Essay Three

QUESTION: How does the literary form of Shakespeare's *Macbeth* reflect his themes of violence and guilt?

ESSAY	COMMENTS
INTRODUCTION As one of Shakespeare's greatest tragedies, *Macbeth* holds a great deal of commentary and insight into notions of violence and guilt. These concerns are at the forefront of the text, as audiences watch the eponymous protagonist and those around him grapple with violent desires and the psychological consequences of pursuing them.[1] By analysing the literary form of the text and chronology of events, we can gain a greater understanding of the ways in which Shakespeare warns audiences of the dangerous capacity for mankind to commit evil acts, and the toll these acts take on both the guilty and the innocent. **PARAGRAPH 1** An important part of *Macbeth's* literary form is the Aristotelian model of the tragic hero and the tragic genre.[2] The first and second acts of the play effectively establish the play's plot, and foreshadow much of the violence that is to come.	1. Try to keep your introductions fairly general – don't list too many characters or specific examples, as this is best saved for your body paragraphs where you can thoroughly unpack evidence and get marks for doing so! 2. Right from the start, this paragraph jumps into linking the structural features of the play with the overarching authorial intent. Literary context is just as important as historical context and is necessary for writing and understanding an essay at a high level.

Furthermore, rather than making it incredibly clear who our relatable and sympathetic hero will be, Shakespeare cleverly undermines Macbeth, as both he and the audience's perception of who is guilty undergo substantial change over the course of the play. Shakespeare also introduces hints of the psychological struggles of guilt with Macbeth and Lady Macbeth's plot to murder Duncan being an example of this as initially the audience are given a sense of what is to come when Macbeth discusses his fear of not being able to sleep in the second scene of the second act after his murder. He warns that "Macbeth does murder sleep" and the initially dismissive Lady Macbeth simply brushes it aside, and in a case of heavy foreshadowing, remarks "a little water clears of this deed". This foreshadowing of Lady Macbeth's insanity introduces the motif of blood,9. Because lots of these examples support similar points, this essay groups quotes together in order to talk about them collectively, thus making the analysis more efficient and effective[3] and idea of the struggle of simply washing off her guilt. Thus, the play establishes a foundation of violence or guilt from the outset, encouraging audiences to observe as these themes and the characters shift over the course of the text.

PARAGRAPH 2
Similarly, the structure of the play also contributes to Shakespeare's explorations of the ramifications of violence. Macbeth's rapid escalation to murder, in particular his attempts on the lives of boys like Fleance and Young Siward,[4] serve to familiarise the audience not only with the evil of his crimes but establish he downfall well in advance of its occurrence.

3. Because lots of these examples support similar points, this essay groups quotes together in order to talk about them collectively, thus making the analysis more efficient and effective!
4. Don't forget that minor characters can be useful supplementary evidence to help you analyse the more important characters like Macbeth, Lady Macbeth, and Macduff.

Beginning with Banquo's murder, two important aspects of Macbeth's relationship with violence are established in the incredibly action-heavy third act. The first is Macbeth using murderers, committing his violence through others, and the second is his willingness to kill those who threaten his position as king. Both foreshadow the brutal slaughter of Lady Macduff and her entire family within the fourth act. This also heralds the inception of the cyclical nature of violence, as by committing theses murders, especially his massacre of the Macduff family, Macbeth incites those to commit violence against him. In this instance, Macbeth's actions are intended to provoke the rage of Macduff, and the structure of the play amplifies his sense of grief, making Macduff's trajectory all the more poignant as in the same establishing fashion and in the same act as Lady Macduff's murder does Macbeth receive the prophecy to "Beware Macduff." Once again, Shakespeare foreshadows to the audience Macbeth's violent end, and uses Macduff's sympathetic sense of guilt[5] for the role his inaction played in his family's demise to subvert our expectations about who the true hero of the play is.

PARAGRAPH 3
Other than the act structure, the themes of violence and guilt are also displayed in the play's form with Shakespeare's use of the tragic hero model[6] established by Aristotle. Macbeth struggles with his guilt to the point where he struggles with his own sanity, thinking he can never wash the guilt off.

5. When discussing the theme of guilt, Macduff is an ideal character to use as a counterpoint, as Macduff feels more guilty for the deaths of his family than Macbeth does, even though Macbeth was the one who ordered the murders.
6. Weaving in literary techniques and structural features is ideal in helping you write a stand-out essay!

Thus, Shakespeare establishes that Macbeth is troubled, a feature of a tragic hero and that guilt may be part of his eventual undoing. By establishing these aspects, the audience is prepared and waiting for what is to come, and when it does during his "tomorrow" soliloquy[7] is it much more impactful that having it simply occur. Macbeth's speech on the futility of life is a powerful character moment and the seeming thematic heart of the text, yet by displaying Macbeth as the central tragic figure at the beginning of the play, his line of "life is but a walking shadow... a tale told by an idiot full of sound and fury signifying nothing" wouldn't carry the same weight. The same can be said about the theme of violence, as by establishing the destructive and almost addictive effect violence seems to have on Macbeth, his one eventual end and the completion of the cycle wouldn't have the same poignancy especially as he is killed by Macduff, the man whose family he had murdered.	7. When, analysing Shakespeare, soliloquies must be referenced when necessary as they are an integral part of the text and offer deep character and thematic insight
CONCLUSION In essence, the literary form of *Macbeth* does a lot more than just keep the pace and drama of the play in check, as it reveals much about its central themes of violence and guilt. By using the structure of the acts and establishing Macbeth as a tragic hero, Shakespeare succeeds in not only offering deep insight into these notions, but also makes them all the more impactful by foregrounding them in his text.[8]	8. This directly links to Shakespeare's authorial context and the essay question.

Essay Four

QUESTION: "The only thing worth writing about is the human heart in conflict with itself" – *William Faulkner*
To what extent do the characters in the text *Macbeth* represent this statement?

ESSAY	COMMENTS
INTRODUCTION Shakespeare's *Macbeth* stands as one of literature's great tragedies and reveals much about the human condition. Many of Macbeth's characters are displayed with incredible and tragic internal conflicts and the full extent the text represents the notion of "the human heart in conflict with itself"[1] can be broken down into three major characters. Macbeth, Lady Macbeth, and Macduff are key to breaking down the impact of the statement and their internal conflicts are what drive the themes and tragedy of the play.	1. If there is a quote in the prompt (either a quote from the play, or from an external source like this one), make an effort to use this quote within your introduction as a springboard for your ideas. 2. Using Macbeth as the primary focus for a character analysis is ideal, and to some extent will be expected by assessors.
PARAGRAPH 1 The most obvious example of a character whose heart is in conflict with themselves is the titular character himself.[2] Macbeth's tale is one of unrelenting ambition and the consequences brought on by such a flaw.	

Though some interpret Macbeth as merely a villain with very little redeeming qualities, this does not do justice to the complexity and depth of Shakespeare's writing. Rather, Macbeth can be analysed as a more conflicted character, reflecting his struggle between the play's two major themes of guilt and ambition. An example of this struggle is within the end of the first act and much of the second act, as Macbeth struggles with even the thought of murdering Duncan to take power. For a character whose central fault is ambition, this early portrayal of Macbeth displays very little of that fault and rather seems like a good man struggling with the morality of doing a bad thing for a position he was seemingly destined for. His declaration that he is "his kinsman and his subject... who should against his murderer shut the door not bear the knife myself"[3] is an example of Macbeth's heart struggling with his ambition.[4] Yet he falters and kills Duncan, with Shakespeare displaying that a side in the struggle of the heart will win. It is does not end here however, as though later it seems Macbeth defeats his guilt and lets his ambition override his morality, there are still hints of the conflict. Right after he murders Duncan and has a moment alone, he wonders if "all great Neptune's ocean" could "wash this blood clean from [his] hand."[5] Thus, Shakespeare through the use of metaphorical blood as a motif of guilt, highlights this conflict between guilt and ambition that manifests itself in Macbeth.

3. Quotes are crucial to any good essay, and you should include a decent amount in every paragraph to help establish your points.
4. Linking your discussion back to the prompt throughout your body paragraphs helps to maintain a sense of relevance.
5. Note that this quote has been modified with the less important information omitted or paraphrased so that the quote better fits into the essay, though still effectively gets the message across.

PARAGRAPH 2

Likewise, Shakespeare also uses Macbeth's downfall to comment on the way guilt causes conflict within the mind and create emotional turmoil for those suffering it. This can even be seen in characters who are only indirectly responsible for the text's tragic outcome, such as Macbeth's foil, Macduff. The two men share many internal conflicts, and reflect to the audience their similarities as well as differences. Though both suffer from guilt, there a few key differences between them and their respective conflicts. Macbeth for one renounces his guilt and ignores the conflict in his heart in order to pursue his ambition, whereas Macduff uses the guilt of leaving his family to die to motivate him to avenge them and to kill Macbeth, announcing "bring thou this fiend of Scotland and myself within my sword's length set him." The second difference is Macbeth's conflict of heart is one done out of selfish desire whereas Macduff's is much more complex. Hence, Macduff's struggle between loyalty to his country over loyalty to his family is a deep and complex one, one that truly tests the values he holds closest to his heart. When Macduff wails "bleed, bleed poor Scotland" in conversations with Malcolm in Act 4, audiences are makde to confront the fact that Macduff cares so deeply about his country that he is willing to commit treason in order to save it, yet his choice leads to the deaths of his family. This epitomises the notion of an inner conflict and compromising of one's own values, and Shakespeare highlights his struggle between family and country to breed both tragedy and a compelling narrative.[6]

6. Again, this is a strong paragraph conclusion that rounds off the discussion by taking the focus back to the core of the prompt and our contention.

PARAGRAPH 3

The most tragic struggle however is that of Lady Macbeth, as the conflict of her ambition and desire is destroyed by the guilt weighing upon her actions to achieve them.[7] It appears that Lady Macbeth goes through various conflicts of the heart throughout the text before he final and tragic battle with one key example being her struggle of her gender identity made evident in her infamous command for spirits to "unsex" her. This highlights Lady Macbeth's desire to renounce her femininity in order to act upon Macbeth's prophecy, and represents a very complex but human struggle. Rather than holding her back though, Shakespeare depicts Lady Macbeth as having the capacity to ignore gender limitations in her patriarchal society, having her devise and execute a plan to murder Duncan. Yet tragically, or perhaps justifiably depending on the audience's perspective, one conflict of heart breeds another as the guilt of her role in Duncan's murder and Macbeth's bloody reign seems to crush her, rendering her into a state of sleep-deprived insanity towards the end of the text, unable to rectify "what's done [that] cannot be undone."[8]

7. This is a highly effective topic sentence that clearly outlines out focus for this paragraph, as well as how this argument builds upon the others we have made so far in this essay.

8. This sentence is an excellent summation of Lady Macbeth's significance in the play, and how her character changes from the start to the end.

CONCLUSION

To this end, *Macbeth*'s characters represent a veritable spectrum of emotions expected from the human heart in conflict with itself. Whether its Macbeth's struggle between morality and ambition, Macduff's between family and country, or Lady Macbeth's with gender, guilt, and desire, it is clear Shakespeare has created characters representative of Faulkner's grand idea of the tragic form.[9]

9. As always, your conclusions can be relatively short and sweet, especially if you're running out of time in test conditions. Just make sure you take the discussion back to the prompt, and reassert your contention or thesis statement.